AN AN

CW00555825

INNE]

Horus the Child, or Harpocrates as he was known to the Græco-Roman World, symbolized silence and secrecy. To the Egyptians, he was the Divine Child. In either case, he represents the Contemplative Child within us (see Introduction).

His finger is to his mouth, and the Greeks thought that this meant that he was admonishing silence. However, it has been pointed out that his finger should really be *in* his mouth, thus depicting, in symbolic form, child-like qualities. It may be that, in the case of this statuette, the end of the first finger, which should be nearer to the mouth, has become somewhat eroded over the years. (The Egyptians always portrayed the various members of the body in their entirety. If only a portion of the finger had been reproduced, they believed that that person would not be complete when he entered the Dwat, or Nether World.)

A silver statuette of Harpocrates, recovered from the Thames at London Bridge.

Department of Prehistoric and Romano-British Antiquities, The British Museum.

Photo: Peter Clayton.

AN ANTHOLOGY
OF
INNER SILENCE

compiled by

CHARLES JESSEL

PELEGRIN TRUST

in association with

PILGRIM BOOKS

TASBURGH · NORWICH · ENGLAND

British Library Cataloguing in Publication Data
An anthology of inner silence.
1. Meditation
I. Jessel, Charles *1924–*   II. Pelegrin Trust
158.12

ISBN 0–946259–37–2

Photoset by Waveney Typesetters, Norwich
and printed in Great Britain at the University Press, Cambridge

Acknowledgements

The idea for this book came from a pamphlet issued by the Bristol Cancer Help Centre, and several of the quotations from that booklet are reproduced by kind permission of the Centre. In addition thanks are due to The White Eagle Publishing Trust for permission to quote extensively from many of their titles and to Messrs Blackie and Son Ltd (Abelard Schumann Ltd) for the many extracts from Hugh l'Anson Fausset's *Fruits of Silence*. In all other instances careful attention has been given to denoting correctly the source of the quotation when it is known to me, and I would like here to acknowledge my indebtedness to the many authors and publishers involved. To those for whom I have not been able to find the original texts, my humble apologies.

I am grateful to numerous friends for their suggestions and advice, and in particular to Ann R. Lay who has, from the other side of the Atlantic, not only provided material but encouraged the project since its inception. Also my thanks are due to Rhoda M. Gaze for her assistance with the index and for the use of her extensive library; and to Robin and Yvonne Helmer for the use of their word processor.

Charles Jessel

To the staff and patients at the
Bristol Cancer Help Centre,
this book is affectionately dedicated.

Foreword

by Pat Pilkington
Co-Founder/Director Cancer Help Centre, Bristol

For over a quarter of a century I have been a dedicated listener to the radio programme Desert Island Discs. It has been remarkable in latter years how many castaways talk with longing of 'Getting away from it all'; away from the noise, the traffic, the telephone. It reflects a deep, intuitive need for at least a measure of peace and quiet in which to recreate and restore ourselves. For noise, especially noise out of control, is a form of torture and is used as such to overwhelm and wear down the wayward resolve of prisoners. Where today in modern society can we go to find a measure of tranquillity to make our lives manageable?

Well, some go fishing! I'm told that more people fish than indulge in any other sport in this country. You can't catch a fish and make a noise! The essence of this sport is silence. What can rest and restore the heart and soul more than hours of quiet on a grassy bank, tranquillized by gently flowing water?

Others of us garden. Gently pottering along with a wheelbarrow, thinking of little, humming a tuneless ditty, unaware of time passing, soothed by Mother Nature, in touch with the earth.

In this excellent book of quotations, one for each day of the year, Sir Charles Jessel presents us with an even simpler method of hushing the noise and stilling the turmoil. We can enter our own inner place of peace in meditation and reflection, guided by the great masters of the past. Are we talking about religious experience? Possibly; not necessarily. But before we can touch the numinous, the ineffable, the eternal, we need to find the still point within ourselves and learn not to be afraid of silence.

For many of us do actually *fear* being alone with ourselves, of being in touch with our thoughts and feelings. Emotions are generally not socially acceptable; anger, jealousy, sorrow, grief are feelings we conceal from public gaze. Most of us just keep busy and assume that our inner needs are being met. But just as we need times of celebration and occasions of ritual to make the changes in our lives, so our every day, and day-to-day experience needs punctuating with times of quiet. Times when we take stock and listen to our higher, wiser self.

Hazrat Inayat Khan (quoted on page 11) tells us that the keynote to a harmonious life is silence. We know that 'silence is golden', of great value. In silence and inner peace we enhance intuition, insight and knowing, and when we enter the silence of meditation with 'expectant gratitude' (see *Moon over Water* by Jessica Macbeth) we can touch deeply into our true Self and the God within.

If you have opened this book and read this far, you are probably already aware that silence, like a quiet pool, can perfectly reflect the sun. However, we need to remind ourselves that for many people silence is something negative to be filled with noise. Whole generations have grown up with this attitude and it is hard to change what we are accustomed to. Wartime evacuees returned swiftly to the bombs of London because they couldn't stand the quiet, couldn't sleep without comforting noise. Today we are accompanied by noise wherever we go; radio, television, walkman, overloud and reverberating 'music'; traffic and machinery around us and overhead. We are busy all day and our minds chatter on in our dreams at night. No wonder that our prisons are overflowing, our mental hospitals full and the level of sickness way beyond what it should be at the end of the twentieth century when medicine has made such giant strides towards treating the body.

The truth may be that much of our disease starts in the mind and soul. Dr. Ann Woolley-Hart says 'Every thought you have can also affect your neuro-endocrine balance' (page 76). There is a direct link from our thoughts and feelings, our moods and state of mind into every single cell in our body. That consciousness can operate on such a microscopic scale has only just been realized by modern medicine. But folk-lore has always said that happy people are well people. 'A merry heart doeth good like medicine' gives Biblical backing to this instinctive knowledge. The immune system stands as guardian to protect our body from disease, but it would seem that each tiny immune cell can also be affected by our thought and mood.

At the Bristol Cancer Help Centre many patients have experienced periods of acute stress prior to their illness. They find very great relief in unburdening their sorrows and expressing their feelings. With deep relaxation and meditation amongst other things, slowly but surely things begin to change. Sleep improves and energy returns. Swami Paramanda says 'What sleep does for our body . . . silence does for our mind and spirit' (page 85). Most of us would not dream of foregoing sleep. Sleep deprivation is a form of torture. How many tortured minds and spirits do we have amongst us today?

Armed with these thoughts we turn to the excellent contents of this book. Each quotation can bring us illumination and guidance as we deliberately set aside quiet moments in which we too can reflect, contemplate and rest, and in the silence heal ourselves.

August 1990

Introduction

What is inner silence? This book tries to find an answer – or rather, many answers. It looks at silence from different angles. Not all silence is the same. Not all silence is even particularly good for us. There can be foolish silence, as one of our authors explains. And we are warned by another that 'the evil spirits enter silently'.

But, hopefully, those who are seeking to calm down their over-active minds and bring their chattering thoughts and turbulent emotions to a standstill will find practical help in these pages. By reading some every night or early morning, they may even bring upon themselves that peace that they are seeking.

An Anthology of Inner Silence is not intended to be read straight through. Rather, it is suggested that a few quotations, or a page or two, be used for meditation or quiet contemplation. Over a period, this can have a soothing, elevating and healing effect on the reader. He, or she, will notice, too, that there is an entry for every day of the year.

It is not pretended that this is in any way a comprehensive collection, if such a thing were possible. But it is an attempt to show the widespread idea of inner silence from many different nations and cultures, and over many centuries of time. It is a unitive idea, and therefore one to which all seekers must ultimately come.

Inner silence is something rather subtle and it is easy to misunderstand its meaning. Some quotations can even lead one astray, although I have tried to omit these from the text as much as possible.

If we can attempt to understand what inner silence *is*, we must also try to see what it is *for*. The two seem to be inextricably linked. One answer, given by William Johnston, is that it is 'the liberation of the true self . . . the natural Child, nurtured by this great love, rises up from the depths of one's being . . . This is the Contemplative Child who is the subject of samadhi and ecstasy and the prayer of quiet'.[1] In other words, 'whosoever shall not receive the kingdom of God as a little child shall in no wise enter therein'.[2]

But, as has been said, this book provides many answers, and I hope that at least some of its contents will guide readers on their way to silence.

[1] William Johnston, *Silent Music*
[2] Luke 18:17

Inner Silence

Be still and know that I am God.

Psalm 46:10

Be still, of course, means calm down, quieten the mind, eliminate all the silly stray thoughts which normally clutter our waking hours.

Howard Kent, 'Yoga'
Encyclopedia of Alternative Medicine and Self-Help

> I am the Dawn, from darkness to release.
> I am the Deep, wherein thy sorrows cease.
> Be still! Be still! and know that I am God.
> Acquaint thyself with Me, and be at peace.
>
> James Rhoades, *Out of the Silence*

Peace I leave with you, my peace I give unto you; not as the world giveth, give I unto you.

John 14:27

1

And after the earthquake a fire; but the Lord was not in the fire; and after the fire a still small voice.

1 Kings 19:12

But thou, when thou prayest, enter into thy closet, and when thou hast shut the door, pray to the Father which is in secret; and thy Father which seeth in secret shall reward thee openly.

Matthew 6:6

. . . the words about entering your closet refer, in characteristically parabolic style, to that secret place within oneself where one can commune alone with God in silence.

Tom Harpur, *For Christ's Sake*

To enter into 'thine inner chamber and shut the door' means to go right into the house of yourself, into the innermost room, and, shutting the door on everything outer, to pray from that inner self that is not a servant of the public or an invented social myth or a seeker of rewards and success and outer praise. It is to pass beyond all connexion with vanity or self-conceit. It is only the internal Man in a man that can obtain response to prayer and can communicate with a higher level. The external worldly side of a man, the pretending man, cannot pray.

Maurice Nicoll, *The New Man*

Commune with your own heart upon your bed, and be still.

Psalm 4:4

It must be borne in mind that the function of meditation is a studious and attentive consideration of Divine things and a passing from one to another, so that the heart may be moved to a certain degree of affection and feeling for them. It is as though one should strike a flint, to draw a spark from it. But contemplation is as though the spark had already been obtained – I mean that the affection and feeling which were sought have now been experienced, and the soul is enjoying it in repose and silence, not by much reasoning and speculation of the understanding, but by simply gazing upon the truth ... What the soul experiences at times like this, what light it rejoices in, what fullness and love and peace it receives, no words can express; for this is that peace that passes all understanding, and all the happiness that this life can attain.

St Peter of Alcántara, *Treatise of Prayer and Meditation*, Part 1, Chapter XII

Silence is not an end in itself but a means to a higher experience.

Friends Book of Discipline

The Lord is my Pace setter; I shall not rush. He makes me stop and rest for quiet intervals; He provides me in ways of efficiency through calmness of mind and His guidance is peace.

Toki Miyashina, *Japanese version of 23rd Psalm*

Deep silence is the medium of real communication. Words, even sincere praise, can exalt the personality of the aspirant while obliterating that silence in which alone the voice of God reveals itself.

Martin Israel, *Summons to Life*

'Solitude', said Father Ravignan, 'is the mother country of the strong and silence is their prayer . . .'

Certainly nothing really great was ever done in this world without the discipline of quiet and recollection. The noblest works, like the temple of Solomon, are brought to perfection in silence . . .

'Silence', says Father Faber, 'has always been the luxury of great holiness which implies that it contains within itself something divine.'

Indeed, St John tells us that it is observed even in heaven: 'There was silence in heaven as it were for half an hour.'

Aloysius Roche, *The Bedside Book of Saints*

Help me, O Lord, to descend into the depths of my being, below my conscious and subconscious self, until I discover my real self, that which is given from Thee, the divine likeness in which I am made and into which I am to grow, the place where your Spirit communes with mine, the spring from which my life rises.

Bishop George Appleton

Only through contemplation and quietness does true intuition arise.

The Secret of the Golden Flower,
A Chinese Book of Life (Translated by R. Wilhelm)

Yoga is the settling of the mind into silence. When the mind has settled, we are established in our essential nature, which is unbounded consciousness.

Patanjali, *The Yoga Sutras*

Absolutely quiet and yet illuminating in a mysterious way, it allows itself to be perceived only by the clear eyed. It is Dharma truly beyond form and sound: it is Tao having nothing to do with words.

D. T. Suzuki, *Manual of Zen Buddhism*

Go placidly amid the noise and haste, and remember what peace there may be in silence.

Desiderata, Old St Paul's Churchyard, Baltimore

If words fail, let us look at other means, and keep quiet until we find we have something to say. In some mysterious way, I think what begins to happen is that not only do we begin to explore silence, but silence begins to explore us.

Wendy Robinson, *Exploring Silence*

Silence is the language of prayer.

Bhagwan Shree Rajneesh, *I Say Unto You*

Only when he has acquired the capacity to create a passive frame of mind can a man hope to hear the voice of the silence, which alone can reveal to him the truths and secrets hidden from him.

P. D. Ouspensky, *A New Model of the Universe*

Nothing in all creation is so like God as silence.

Meister Eckhart, *Sermons and Treatises*, Vol. 1

Never flaunting the omnipresence, the Lord is heard only in the immaculate silences.

Parahamsa Yogananda, *Autobiography of a Yogi*

Wherefore the most profound and divine theologians say that God is better honoured and loved by silence than by words, and better seen by closing the eyes to images than by opening them; and therefore the negative theology of Pythagoras and Dionysius is so celebrated and placed above the demonstrative theology of Aristotle and the Scholastics.

Geordano Bruno, *Eroici Furori*

. . . three degrees of silence – silence of the mouth, silence of the mind and silence of the will. To refrain from idle talk is hard; to quieten the gibbering of memory and imagination is much harder; hardest of all is to still the voice of craving and aversion within the will.

Aldous Huxley, *The Perennial Philosophy*

Drop Thy still dews of quietness
Till all our strivings cease.
Take from our souls the strain and stress
And let our ordered lives confess
The beauty of Thy peace

Breathe through the heats of our desire
Thy coolness and thy balm;
Let sense be dumb, let flesh retire;
Speak through the earthquake, wind and fire,
O still small voice of calm!

Hymn, J. G. Whittier (1807–1892)

Anyone who thinks his time is too valuable to spend keeping quiet will eventually have no time for God or his brother, but only for himself and his own follies.

Dietrich Bonhoeffer

Silence is the audience chamber of God.
Michael Wynn Parker, *Healing and the Wholeness of Man*

But there exists an inner silence in which the necessary awareness can be cultivated. The more silent, in this sense, that I or you or anyone can be, the more intense and effective will be our action.

Apa Pant, *A Moment in Time*

The secret of meditation is silence: no repetitions, no affirmations, no denials – just acknowledgement of God's allness, and then the deep, deep silence which announces God's presence. The deeper the silence the more powerful is the meditation.

Joel S. Goldsmith, *Practising the Presence*

Those who know do not talk.

Lao Tsu, *Tao Te Ching*

The sage goes about doing nothing, teaching no talking.
                                    Lao Tsu, *Tao Te Ching*

Silence is the element in which great things fashion themselves.
                          Thomas Carlyle, *Sartor Resartus*

An[other] effective technique in developing a peaceful mind is the daily practise of silence.
        Norman Vincent Peale, *The Power of Positive Thinking*

God is known only when the human mind is at rest.
                    Joel S. Goldsmith, *The Art of Meditation*

No man or woman of my acquaintance who knows how to practise silence and does it has ever been sick to my knowledge.
                                              Starr Daily

He who knows his soul (inner self) daily retires to the region of Swarga (the heavenly realm) in his own heart.
                          Brihad Aranyaka Upanishad

9

In order to form a habit of conversing with God continually, I make it my business only to persevere in His holy presence, when I keep myself by simple attention and a general fond regard to God, which I may call an actual presence of God, or to speak better, an habitual silent and secret conversation of the soul with God.

Brother Lawrence, *The Practice of the Presence of God*

. . . only in complete quietude of body and mind may the voice of the Master within be heard.

Geoffrey Hodson, *The Concealed Wisdom of World Mythology*

Pearl-shell, what gives you your precious contents? Silence: for my lips were closed.

An Indian Poet

I come to those who listen for my step. Seek ye the silence . . . draw within.

Anon., *The Way of the Servant*

In ancient mysteries the newly admitted brother had to sit in silence, he was not allowed to walk or speak; he had to be, to work and to watch, because one cannot enter the fifth kingdom, or climb the mountain of Capricorn, until there has been restraint of speech and control of thought.

Alice A. Bailey, *The Labours of Hercules*

10

One must listen to the silence, even if nothing speaks and nothing answers, even if everything seems stupid and inert. Silence is always fruitful but its fruit often appears outside one's own periods of silence, at the most unexpected moments. Silence is a well into which falls the universe, the void into which the Spirit is drawn. But the consciousness which is aroused at such moments may remain obscure for a while longer, and the Wisdom which they bring forth in the depths of the heart may take time to rise to the surface.

Isha Schwaller de Lubicz, *The Opening of the Way*

We must daily retire in silence far into the depths of our spirits and experience the real life within us.

Rabindranath Tagore

The keynote to harmonious life is silence.

Hazrat Inayat Khan, *Healing and the Mind World*

Silence is the earliest fruit to ripen when you have learned control of the senses and the three lower states, the physical, emotional and mental. It is the well of wisdom containing all treasures, the locus of all knowledge.

Isha Schwaller de Lubicz, *The Opening of the Way*

Once I asked my spiritual teacher what was the sign of knowing God. He said: 'Not those who call out the Name of God, but whose silence says it.'

Hazrat Inayat Khan, *Healing and the Mind World*

In Capricorn he [Hercules] becomes the Initiate, and this stage is always impossible until illusion has been overcome and the power of silence has been achieved.

Alice A. Bailey, *The Labours of Hercules*

Silence practised in meditation is something apart, but silence means that we shall consider every word and every action we do; that is the first lesson. If there is a meditative person, he has learned to use that silence naturally in everyday life. The one who has learned silence in everyday life has already learned to meditate.

Hazrat Inayat Khan, *Healing and the Mind World*

Guidance such as Mine comes in the quiet of the soul's silence, not in the outer information of the pages of a book.

Anon., *The Way of the Servant*

Be silent, and thou will be happy. Do not be garrulous. The dwelling of God, its abomination is clamor. Pray thou with a living heart, all the words of which are hidden, and he will do what thou needest, he will hear what thou sayest, and he will accept thy offering.

'The Instruction of Ani' [Egypt 1100–800 B.C.],
Ancient Near Eastern Texts, Princeton

Chasi (Syriac)   = pious
Chasa (Hebrew) = silent
Chassidism   = the silent ones who meditate on mysteries.

Word Definitions

Mertseger or Merseger: a Theban goddess who was closely associated with Osiris and represented silence.

Max Shapiro and Rhoda Hendricks,
A Dictionary of Mythologies

For so He giveth Himself to His beloved in quietness.
Dorothy Kerin, *Chapel House Notes*, Burrswood

Abide still, O my people, and take thy rest, for thy quietness shall come.

II Esdras 2:24

13

One must never forget the ancient maxim: 'the best medicament is silence'.

Abraham Joshua Heschel, *Quest for God*

Verily we created man, and we know what his soul whispereth to him, for we are nearer to him than the jugular vein.

The Kur'an 1:15

The Four Quiet States:
1. A quiet environment.
2. A quiet body.
3. A quiet receptive attitude.
4. A quiet mind – in the sense of being 'unbusy' but alert and poised.

Ludi How and Michael Brookman, Cancer Help Centre, Bristol, 1983

Exert yourself to restrain your speech.

'Counsels of Wisdom' (Akkadian Wisdom Literature, c. 2500 B.C.) *Ancient Near Eastern Texts*, Princeton

For Godsake hold your tongue and let me love.

John Donne, *The Canonization*

Right speech comes out of silence, and right silence comes out of speech ... Silence is nothing else but waiting for God's Word and coming from God's Word with a blessing. But everybody knows that this is something that needs to be practised and learned, in these days when talkativeness prevails. Real silence, real stillness, really holding one's tongue come only as the sober consequence of spiritual stillness.

Dietrich Bonhoeffer, *Life Together*

None speaketh surely but would gladly keep silence if he might.

Thomas à Kempis

There is a time to keep silent and a time to speak.

Ecclesiastes 3:7

Out of the silence that is peace a resonant voice shall arise. And this voice will say: It is not well; thou hast reaped, now thou must sow. And knowing this voice to be the silence itself thou wilt obey.

Mabel Collins, *Light on the Path*

Then, with reason armed with resolution, let the seeker quietly lead the mind into the Spirit and let all his thoughts be silence.

The Bhagavad Gita 6:25

. . . the person who has a quiet and calm mind. Such a person is at peace with himself and with the whole world. His quietness is undisturbed by outside influences, and in that quietness comes the solution to his problems. He has learned how to control thought and imagination, and how to put them to constructive use.

Philip M. Chancellor,
Handbook of the Bach Remedies (White Chestnut)

To be still and confident in the presence of God opens our minds to the Divine Wisdom: to the Soul Science, which is not of this world.

In quietness and in confidence we are taught the great and mighty things of the Spirit.

H. B. Jeffery, *The Principle of Healing*

One must remain calm, indifferent and in a passive mental state, without any preconceived ideas, and submit to reality without trying to distort it.

Abbé Mermet, *Principles and Practice of Radiesthesia*

Meditation is the emptying of the mind of the activity of the self.

Krishnamurti, *On Meditation*, 1973

To obtain the pure silence necessary for the disciple, the heart and emotions, the brain and its intellectualisms, have to be put aside.

Mabel Collins, *Light on the Path*

Do nought with the body but relax; shut firm the mouth and silent remain; empty your mind and think of nought. Like a hollow bamboo rest at ease your body. Giving not nor taking, put your mind at rest.

Mahamudra is like a mind that clings to nought.

Thus practising, in time you will reach Buddhahood.

Tilopa, *The Song of Mahamudra*

In order to enter the stillness, it is necessary to raise one's intelligence to a higher degree of consciousness. The stillness is neither a passive, inert state, nor trance, in my experience. When achieved it is a lucid work of intense activity.

Geraldine Cummins, *Swan on a Black Sea*

All that is more mysterious is more deep. What all the prophets and masters have done in all ages is to express that mystery in words, in deeds, in thought, in feelings; but most of the mystery is exposed by them in silence.

Hazrat Inayat Khan, *Character Building and Personality*

Word of God's own, from silence proceeding . . .
Ignatius of Antioch, *Letters*

The greatest gift a healer can give to his client is to be at peace himself.
Dr Edward Bach

There are of course grades of this peace, for it is not given to many to reach the peace that passeth understanding.
Michael Wetzler,
'Perspectives of Health, Healing and Wholeness',
in *Healing*, edited Lorna St Aubyn

The fount of prayer is in the heart; by thought, not words, the heart is carried up to God, where it is blest. Then let us pray. They prayed but not a word was said; but in that holy silence every heart was blest.
Levi, *The Aquarian Gospel of Jesus the Christ*

My beloved is the mountains, the solitary wooded valleys, strange islands . . . silent music.
St John of the Cross, *Ascent of Mount Carmel*

18

Silentium mysticum (Latin), mystical silence. This term is used in Christian mystical theology to denote a state of quiet beyond conceptual thought in which the spirit rests in a sense of God's presence.

William Johnston, *Silent Music*

In the meditation of the great religions one makes progress by going beyond concepts, beyond images, beyond reasoning, thus entering a deeper state of consciousness or enhanced awareness that is characterised by profound silence.

William Johnston, *Silent Music*

In Christianity it is called contemplation or, in its earlier stages, the prayer of quiet. In Zen it is called san'nai, which is a Japanese rendering of samadhi. Elsewhere it is called one-pointedness.

William Johnston, *Silent Music*

. . . among the many kinds of interior silence are some that are unhealthy. It is well said in Japan that any clown can tell the difference between wise talk and foolish talk; but it takes a good master to distinguish wise silence and foolish silence.

William Johnston, *Silent Music*

They were called Magi, because they glorified God in
silence and in a low voice.

Book of Seth, 6th Century
Quoted by Fulcanelli, *Le Mystère des Cathédrales*

The superior work you have done so industriously in
quietness should be applied when you are submerged in
the tumult of your daily life.

Garma Chang, *The Practice of Zen*

Meditation is a silence. A deep, deep silence. You must
consciously approach it in the silence.

Chan, spirit guide to Ivy Northage,
Spiritual Realisation

Be still. Learn to stand silent, quiet and unafraid. I, at
the centre, AM. Look up along the line and not along the
many lines . . . These hold thee prisoner. Be still.

Ancient Aphorism

When no-mind is sought after by a mind, that is making
it a particular object of thought. There is only testimony
of silence; it goes beyond thinking.

Huang-Po

Twofold is the meaning of silence. One, the abstinence from speech. Two, inner silence, the absence of self concern, stillness. One may articulate words in his voice and yet be inwardly silent. One may abstain from uttering any sound and yet be over-bearing.

Abraham Joshua Heschel, *Quest for God*

Be silent all flesh before the Lord.

Zechariah 2:13

We reach into the Light and bring it down to meet the need. We reach into the Silent Place and bring from thence the gift of understanding.

The Master Djwhal Khul

The Father uttered one Word; that Word is His Son, and He utters Him for ever in everlasting silence; and in silence the soul has to hear it.

St John of the Cross

The spiritual life is nothing else but the working of the Spirit of God within us, and therefore our own silence must be a great part of our preparations for it, and much speaking or delight in it will be often no small hindrance of that good which we can only have from hearing what the Spirit and voice of God speaketh within us.

William Law

When you reach the centre of Consciousness, you find a complete stillness – a deep well of silence. It is not power, since there is nothing for it to be a power to, or over: It just IS.

Joel Goldsmith, *The Infinite Way*

While you repose, endeavour to cultivate this attitude of silence of intellect and receptivity. But take care. The mere suppression of thoughts only makes them rebound! The emptiness of your mind must be a 'positive emptiness' – not a negative one. An active relaxation is necessary – an attitude of listening with your heart and mind! I realise that this is quite difficult in the beginning but success is assured through sincere desire and perseverance.

Albert Pauchard, *The Other World*

There is no longer any room in our existence for quietude. We say we clamour for it, but when we achieve it we don't know what to do with it. In Hunza, people find time to meditate in the silence of their homes or in the little mosques which stand in each valley.

Renée Taylor, *Hunza Health Secrets*

For whereas speaking detracts, silence and work collect the thoughts and strengthen the spirit. As soon therefore as a person understands what has been said to him for his own good, there is no further need to hear or to discuss; but to set himself in earnest to practise what he has learnt with silence and attention, in humility, charity and contempt of self.

St John of the Cross

You cannot practise too rigid a fast from the charms of worldly talk.

Fenelon

A dog is not considered a good dog because he is a good barker.
A man is not considered a good man because he is a good talker.

Chuang Tsu

The virtue of Binah is said to be silence, and its vice Avarice ... Silence indicates receptivity. If we are silent we can listen, and so learn; but if we are talking, the gates of entrance to the mind are closed.

Dion Fortune, *The Mystical Quabalah*

. . . because of this inner state of eternal contentment the mind of a yogi abides in silence.

Maharishi Mahash Yogi,
Commentary on the Bhagavad Gita

For supreme happiness comes to the yogi whose mind is deep in peace, in whom the spur to activity is stilled, who is without blemish and has become one with Brahman.

Krishna in *The Bhagavad Gita*

. . . Silence is above all a quality of the heart that can stay with us even in our conversation with others. It is a portable cell that we carry with us wherever we go. From it we speak to those in need and to it we return after our words have born fruit. It is in this portable cell that we find ourselves immersed in divine silence.

Fr Henri Nouwen, *The Way of the Heart*

Silence is an indispensable discipline in the spiritual life. Silence is solitude practised in action.

Fr Henri Nouwen, *The Way of the Heart*

Where can I find a man who has forgotten words? He is the one I would like to talk to.

Chuang Tsu

Keep silence, thou who art admitted to the secret rites.
Chaldean Oracles (Kroll 55)

And Jesus stood still, and called them, and said: What will ye that I should do unto you? They say unto him: Lord, that our eyes may be opened.
Matthew 20:32

Keep silence before me O islands; and let the people renew their strength.
Isaiah 41:1

The 'silence' he learns to keep is a quite different matter. He [the candidate for Initiation] acquires this fine quality in regard to things of which he used previously to speak, especially in regard to the manner in which he spoke . . . The only obstacle to communication in this field is lack of understanding by a recipient.
Rudolf Steiner, *Knowledge of the Higher Worlds*

As you go about in the world, do not forget those silent moments when, in the quiet of your inmost sanctuary, you have felt a spiritual power, the touch of angels' wings ... Do your best quietly and you will be working in accordance with that divine law which will 'make crooked places straight', and restore harmony and health.

White Eagle, *Heal Thyself*

There was perfect discipline, and a most profound silence. All hearts were united and each man forgave his enemies.

Kenneth Clark, 'The building of Chartres Cathedral', *Civilisation*

But you who are born of the mountains and the forests and the seas can find their prayer in your heart. And if you listen in the stillness of the night your shall hear them saying in silence: Our God, who art our winged self, it is thy will in us that willeth.

Kahlil Gibran, *The Prophet*

In this time of stillness, the higher or inner you will know exactly what to do for your inner perfecting and outer and inner growth. Be still and trust in the God within.

Jessie K. Crum, *The Art of Inner Listening*

. . . the simple problem which faces the aspirant to Meditation. He has to learn to produce stillness in his body, emotions and mind, so that together they constitute one calm chalice, which can receive and reflect truth as a quiet pool can perfectly reflect the sun. In such quietness also the auditory nerve can distinguish the 'still small voice' of real consciousness.

Vera Stanley Alder, *The Fifth Dimension*

The highest form of worship is that of silence and hope.

Ibn Gabriol, *The Choice of Pearls*

Krishnamurti . . . is constantly teaching: 'It is only when the totality of the mind is still, that the creative, the nameless, comes into being'.

. . . The goal of mind control is important: the particular method used to reach the goal is not . . . When the restless mind is finally controlled and held still, the higher levels of our being have a chance to reveal themselves.

Raynor C. Johnson, *A Religious*
[Krishnamurti died in 1985]   *Outlook for Modern Man*

Truth is always realised in silence. When your inner talk has stopped, then it is realised.

Bhagwan Shree Rajneesh, *Tao. The Three Treasures*

It is the inner vision and the still, small voice which is apprehended in full consciousness, and not the apparition or the trumpet of the seance room in trance condition.

Aubrey Westlake, *The Pattern of Health*

You do not serve Him in the stillness and in the quiet; you are fed in the stillness and in the quiet, and then He expects you to get up from the table and use the food that you have taken in by applying it to other people, by putting it to work in other lives.

Paul Solomon, *Love One Another*

... in a grove on three sides of which stand three temples, dedicated to Wisdom, Reason and Nature. Thither, the three Genii lead Tamino, and leave him with the advice that he 'be silent, patient and persevering'.

Kobbé's Opera Book, Mozart, The Magic Flute

To re-align ourselves with energy requires a complete stilling of our habitual responses to external and internal stimuli.

Lawrence Blair, *Rhythms of Vision*

'And what are the seven lessons that man must know, O Mother?' And She made response: 'Pleasure is the first and easiest, Pain is the next, Hate is the third, Illusion the fourth, Truth the fifth, Love is sixth and Peace must be learnt at the end.'

Paul Brunton, *A Search in Secret Egypt*

This new knowledge was not arrived at out of penetrating logical thought; indeed, in the meditation through which it was reached, every activity of mind and body had to be stilled. It was as if one sat silently before the facts of the world of sense experience, until the eyes of the spirit were opened to their secrets.

A. P. Shepherd, D.D., *A Scientist of the Invisible*

This state of 'one-pointedness', as it has been called, constitutes an essential condition for perfect contemplation; outwardly the being is quiet, with the mind wholly withdrawn from all objects of sense around it; its gaze is 'turned inward' – to use a common Tibetan expression – and wholly absorbed in the vision; but that apparent stillness, which the ignorant mistake for inactivity, actually represents the most real and intense state of activity conceivable, for it is indistinguishable from the Activity of Heaven itself.

Marco Pallis, *The Active Life*

This is the way healing work is done: go within; get quiet; become still until the peace that passeth understanding descends. True spiritual healing is not something that takes place in the body or in one's affairs; it takes place in the consciousness of the individual as the soul is opened.

Joel Goldsmith, *Practising the Presence*

Entering the silence is a good thing: it is really entering the inner silence of the inner sanctuary where the Divine Spirit abides in fulness. To misuse this inward power for selfish and material ends, and for forcing our human will upon life, so as to make it conform to what we think it ought to be, is a crime of the first magnitude, which can result only in ultimate failure and disaster.

Henry Thomas Hamblin, *Within You is the Power*

... during the healing process silence should be maintained in the mind as well as vocally.

C. Maxwell Cade, *Wrekin Trust Lecture*

Lord, make me an instrument of Thy peace.

The Prayer of St Francis

The condition, or requirement, for the conscious functioning of both [intuition and the illumined mind] is, first of all, an inner silence, achieved in and maintained by receptive meditation. As one teacher has said, '. . . the cultivation of a technique of silence is of incalculable value . . . In the silence power is generated, problems are solved and important recognitions are registered. In the silence sensitivity can be developed and the ability to respond to subjective impressions.'

Sundial House, *Meditation for the New Age*

A great and impressive silence reigned as they [The Essenes] worked in harmony with nature creating veritable kingdoms of heaven in their brotherhoods.

Edmond Bordeaux Szekely, *From Enoch to the Dead Sea Scrolls*

All the proportions of life change in the silence. The things of time shrink in scale by the side of the things eternal.

Cyril Hepher, *The Fellowship of Silence*

Gold is the symbol of the hidden wisdom, which is understood in the silence of the heart – an idea which has come down to us in the saying 'Silence is Golden'.

Vera W. Reid, *Towards Aquarius*

... there have been in all religious traditions schools of so-called quietism, and their voices can still be heard today: 'Be absolutely still! Empty the mind! Erase all thoughts from your consciousness! Blot out everything! Stop thinking! And this is mysticism.'

But this is not mysticism, oriental or occidental. This is nonsense.

William Johnston, *The Inner Eye of Love*

It is not a question of thinking and reasoning and logic, but of transcending all thinking and entering what modern people call an altered state of consciousness. Here one is in darkness, in emptiness, in the cloud of unknowing precisely because one does not know through clear images and thoughts nor with the eye of the body. There is a great inner silence, but it is a rich silence – and that is why we call it silent music. There is conceptual darkness; but the inner eye is filled with light.

William Johnston, *The Inner Eye of Love*

Love is the motivation and driving force behind the mystical journey – it is precisely love that leads one beyond thought and images and concepts into the world of silence. The inner eye is now the eye of love. If this seems difficult to understand, it may be helpful to reflect that human love often has the same effect. Profound human love may draw the lovers into a state of deep, unitive silence where thoughts and concepts become unnecessary and even superfluous yet where the inner eye, the eye of love, penetrates powerfully to the core of the other's being. Such human union is similar to (perhaps in certain cases it is identical with) the mystical loving silence about which the medievals write.

William Johnston, *The Inner Eye of Love*

In contemplation God teaches the soul very quietly and secretly, without it knowing how, without the sound of words, and without the help of any bodily faculty, in silence and quietude, in darkness to all sensory and natural things. Some spiritual persons call this knowing by unknowing.

St John of the Cross, *Spiritual Canticle* 39:12

What precisely is this silence which is uniting you – Christians and Buddhists? And I would answer, first of all it is our common nature. When we sit together in silent meditation, just being, we are experiencing our true selves at the existential level. We are all doing the same thing: just being. And this gives birth to a powerful unity.

William Johnston, *The Inner Eye of Love*

33

In the united stillness of a truly 'gathered' meeting there is a power known only by experience, and mysterious even when most familiar.

Caroline Stephen, Quaker Strongholds

Be silent, that the Lord who gave thee language may speak. For as He fashioned a door and a lock, He has also made a key.

Jalalud din Rumi, Divani Shamsi Tabriz

The world would be happier if men had the same capacity to be silent that they have to speak.

Benedictus de Spinosa, Ethica II

When the disposition is similar to that of the [evil] spirits, they enter silently, as one coming into his own house when the doors are open.

St Ignatius of Loyola, The Spiritual Exercises

Silence is a true friend who never betrays.

Confucius

I regret often that I have spoken; never that I have been silent.

Publilius Syrus, Sententiae, c. 50 B.C.

Through the cultivation of the silence you will move about your daily tasks more quietly, not chatter so much (and certainly less about yourself), become less tense and more relaxed, and meet your problems and responsibilities with less effort and strain, because every moment you are claiming and using the gifts of the silence.

Clare Cameron, *Entering The Silence*

So it is that every spiritual healing is the result of one individual sitting in the silence, quietly, peacefully waiting, and then the Spirit comes through the consciousness of that one – the voice thunders in the silence, and the earth melts.

Joel S. Goldsmith, *The Thunder of Silence*

How to bring forth the Relaxation Response:
1. A Quiet Environment.
2. A Mental Device.
3. A Passive Attitude.
4. A Comfortable Position.

Herbert Benson, *The Relaxation Response*

The Emperor asked: 'And what is meant by *shen*, the spirit? What is the spirit?' Ch'i Po answered: 'Let me discuss *shen*, the spirit. What is the spirit? The spirit cannot be heard with the ear. The eye must be brilliant of perception and the heart must be open and attentive and then the spirit is suddenly revealed through one's own consciousness. It cannot be expressed through the mouth; only the heart can express all that can be looked upon. If one pays close attention one may suddenly know it but one can just as suddenly lose this knowledge. But *shen*, the spirit, becomes clear to man as though the wind had blown away the cloud. Therefore one speaks of it as the spirit.'

The Yellow Emperor's Classic of Internal Medicine,
Before 300 B.C. Translated: Ilza Veith

All minds are joined. Therefore, all healing is self healing. Our inner peace will of itself pass to others once we accept it for ourselves.

Gerald G. Jampolsky, *Teach Only Love*

... it is possible for anyone to quietly listen to his inner guide, who will teach him the way to freedom. Love knows no place it cannot go and no person it cannot bring rest.

Gerald G. Jampolsky, *Teach Only Love*

Stone walls do not a prison make
Nor iron bars a cage;
Minds innocent and quiet take
That for a hermitage;
If I have freedom in my love,
And in my soul am free;
Angels alone, that soar above,
Enjoy such liberty.

Richard Lovelace, *To Althea. From Prison*

The method by which an individual can attain direct
spiritual awareness, God-consciousness, will be peculiar
to himself, though certain general, age-old rules have
been enunciated. The psalmist said: 'Be still and know
that I am God.' ... Through sacred chanting, as also
through silent contemplation excluding every thought,
he may find and know the God within, the inner ruler
immortal 'seated in the heart of all beings'. (Bhavagad
Gita)
Geoffrey Hodson, *The Hidden Wisdom in the Holy Bible*,
Vol. 1

The ear of corn was the central symbol of the Eleusinian
Mysteries. 'There was exhibited as the great, the
admirable, the most perfect object of mystic contemplation an ear of corn that had been reaped in silence.'
(Philosophoumena)

J. C. Cooper, *An Illustrated Encyclopaedia of
Traditional Symbols*

Physical stillness is the first gateway to mental stillness ... Go to the same quiet spot or room every day, occupy the same chair or sit in the same bed each time. Sit upright and do not recline on your back. Thus the body learns to respond automatically until it becomes non-resistant to the invading influence of the Soul.

Paul Brunton, *The Secret Path*

... as the mind begins to quiet itself, our intuitive and holistic abilities may become more evident, as they probably were in our ancestors, who relied more on intuition rather than logic for their understanding of the world.

Anthony J. Sattilaro, *Recalled By Life*

To repeat continuously, 'Be still and know that I am God' is nothing but suggestive therapy, nothing but affirmation and denial used to hypnotize oneself. It is not spiritual practice, it is not spiritual power ... The pre-requisite for the hearing of the still small voice, for the actual experience of the Christ, is to prepare ourselves by study, meditation, and by mingling with others on the spiritual path.

Joel S. Goldsmith, *The Art of Meditation*

The consciousness of God's presence is developed by patience and perseverance, in quietness and stillness, and by abstaining from the use of mental power or physical might, so that the Spirit may function.

Joel S. Goldsmith, *The Art of Meditation*

The still mind of the Sage is the mirror of heaven and earth, the glass of all things.

Chuang Tsu

The rose ... typifies silence and secrecy, *sub rosa*, a rose being hung, or depicted, in council chambers to symbolize secrecy or discretion.

J. C. Cooper, *An Illustrated Encyclopaedia of Traditional Symbols*

... the key to freedom lies symbolically in the non-rotating centre of the circle – the hub of the wheel. Christ in this imagery is the thirteenth point at the centre of the circle of twelve disciples, as Arthur is at the Round Table of Knights. Only at the centre is the stillness of the Spirit.

Herbert Whone, *Church, Monastery, Cathedral*

Grieve not when I am Silent, and joy not in the hearing of My Voice. But know that I am Silence and the Sound.

Anon., *The Way of the Servant*

For ah! we know not what each other says
These things and I; in sound I speak –
Their sound is but their stir, they speak by silences.

Francis Thompson, *The Hound of Heaven*

The seat of silence should be the depths of our being, and
that 'being' only utters something true and profound
when it comes from that silence, and is its expression . . .
It is in that silence that He speaks to us, and bids us listen
to Him.

A Carthusian, *They Speak by Silences*

Within, my child, within. My voice is in the heart, and
breaketh not the lesser silences. Beware of voices that
assail the ear. Rest silently, with body stilled, with senses
quieted and mind subdued: let go thyself and thou shalt
know thyself, awake alert – then seek, and ye shall find.

Anon., *The Way of the Servant*

When we meditate we are allowing our spiritual
consciousness to rise and release itself from the prison of
the physical barriers and go forth on our behalf for
replenishment. This is best done in complete silence. As
we enter into this silence it becomes increasingly
powerful, so that even our very thoughts are still.

Chan, spirit guide to Ivy Northage,
Spiritual Realisation

It is in silence that we shall come to understand the supreme mystery of Love that has no comparison.

F. Hadland Davis, *The Persian Mystics*

> Elected silence, sing to me,
> And beat upon my whorled ear,
> Pipe to me pastures still and be
> The music that I care to hear.

Gerard Manley Hopkins, *The Habit of Perfection*

Silence is the fence around wisdom.

Hebrew Proverb

Silence is the absolute poise or balance of body, mind and spirit. The man who preserves his selfhood is ever calm and unshaken by the storms of existence – not a leaf, as it were, astir on the tree; not a ripple upon the surface of the shining pool – his, in the mind of the unlettered sage, is the ideal attitude and conduct of life.

If you ask him: 'What is silence?' he will answer: 'It is the Great Mystery! The holy silence is His voice!' If you ask: 'What are the fruits of silence?' he will say: 'They are self-control, true courage and endurance, patience, dignity and reverence. Silence is the cornerstone of character.'

Ohiyesa, Santee Dakota North American Indian,
Touch the Earth

The silence of the tongue is merely when it is not incited to evil speech; the silence of the entire body is when all its senses are unoccupied, the silence of the soul is when there are not ugly thoughts bursting forth within it; the silence of the mind is when it is not reflecting on any harmful knowledge or wisdom; the silence of the spirit is when the mind ceases even from stirrings caused by spiritual beings and all its movements are stirred solely by Being, at the wondrous awe of the silence which surrounds Being.

John the Solitary, Syrian Monk c. 5th Century,
On Prayer

Empty yourself of everything.
Let the mind rest at peace.
The ten thousand things rise and fall while the Self watches their return.
They grow and flourish and then return to the source.
Returning to the source is stillness, which is the way of nature.

Lao Tsu, *Tao Te Ching*

Keep silence, that you may hear him speaking
Words unutterable by tongue in speech.
Keep silence, that you may hear from that Sun
Things inexpressible in books and discourses.
Keep silence, that the Spirit may speak to you . . .

Jalalud din Rumi, *Masnavi I Masnavi*

I sometimes think that while it is noble of us to investigate these recondite and difficult thoughts [of infinity, etc.] because they raise us to higher levels of thinking and enlarge our minds, I sometimes think that I must agree with the ancient sage who said that the answers, the realest answer, the most real answer, to such problems is found in the silence.

G. de Purucker, *Wind of the Spirit*

A guardian angel, which forms a separate category in the world of angels, has the task of being a messenger to those who have descended into time. He also has a duty to protect and carefully guide us, and often he warns us. His signals are probably received by the right side of the brain. But we only hear them when we are quiet inside.

Hans C. Moolenburgh, *A Handbook of Angels*

We may close our eyes against the outside world, but our brains are full of images, which the outside world has impressed upon them and of notions or incidents which are in the forefront or the background of our memory. We do not need to summon them. They form the grain and tissue of that transitory but tenacious self which we suppose our selves to be. Only as that self dissolves do they lose their power over us. The tyranny they still exert when we try to maintain an inner silence shows how far we are as yet from wholly desiring the dissolution of that self.

Hugh l'Anson Fausset, *Fruits of Silence*

Only by finding the kernel of true being in ourselves and by grounding our life in it can we enter into communion with the true being in everything else. It is to find this hidden kernel that we invoke the silence. And the silence becomes real to us as we cease to identify ourselves either pleasurably or painfully with our feelings and thoughts.

Hugh l'Anson Fausset, *Fruits of Silence*

We turn to the silence because we instinctively know that we are nearer to this essence of our being when we are still and receptive than at any other time and that until we have learnt to open our hearts to it and to keep them open, false tension in thought and act will continue to demoralize us.

Hugh l'Anson Fausset, *Fruits of Silence*

Beloved, come with me away from the fears and disturbances of your external life into this secret place of your being which is my home and where you meet me face to face. Here only may you know peace, but here always it is known by the doing of my Father's will.

Margery Eyre, *The Seeker and The Finding*

If we abandon altogether the arguments and counter arguments in which our restless minds take such a pleasure, and so become still and alert to reality, we shall find a deeper faculty of knowledge opening in us, that 'Golden Flower' of intuitive awareness, in which the conflict of doubt and belief, characteristic of the mental selfhood, is resolved and the true polarity established.

Hugh l'Anson Fausset, *Fruits of Silence*

The Word proceeds from silence, and we strive to find Him in His Source. This is because the silence here in question is not a void or a negation but, on the contrary, Being at Its fullest and most fruitful plenitude.

A Carthusian, *They Speak by Silences*

Silence is more musical than any song.
Christina Georgina Rossetti, *Rest*

Silence is as full of potential wisdom and wit as the unhewn marble of great sculpture.
Aldous Huxley, *Point Counter Point*

This intuitive or contemplative faculty, which we are to cultivate, is quite distinct from our ordinary brain-thinking. Its insight is of another order than logical acuteness. It is this faculty by which we can respond to the inspiration of the eternal Word, which speaks in the silence of the soul.

Hugh l'Anson Fausset, *Fruits of Silence*

Silence can open a door on a new dimension of reality. It is like finding a trap door or a secret passage, giving a way out of our usual ego-dominated existence. Where there seemed to be only an endless, gray alley of concrete and mortar, or a prison of velvet walls with scarcely air to breathe, in silence suddenly we find ourselves in open country.

Morton T. Kelsey, *The Other Side of Silence*

I like the silent church before the service begins, better than any preaching.

Ralph Waldo Emerson, *Self Reliance*

We may wish ... to name the presence which is the silence itself the better to relate ourselves to It and to articulate Its mysteries. But the silence has taught us that It is immeasurably beyond any name which men have given to It and any form in which imagination may clothe It.

Hugh l'Anson Fausset, *Fruits of Silence*

... as we immerse ourselves in the silence, we draw nearer to that greater Consciousness which creates us in the likeness of Itself and knows Itself in us.

Hugh l'Anson Fausset, *Fruits of Silence*

The heart which in the silence will begin to open as we concentrate our attention on it and, free from all distraction, pray only to enter into it, is not the physical heart, though that is, as it were, a valve of it. It is the eternal heart of life itself, the sun in that inward heaven which we are here to realize ... This is the heart, centred within us, which we need to enter in the silence.

Hugh l'Anson Fausset, *Fruits of Silence*

You cannot still the mind until it has naturally reached the point of stillness. Man's mind is the transformer, the mediator that moves, guides, attracts or repels the essence of God. The intellect may tune the faculties but in itself it cannot attract God for God is moved by the quality of the heart. The need for perfection motivates the search for wisdom. But wisdom is first given by God in such obvious form that it would insult the intellect.

Margaret, Viscountess Long of Wraxall,
Let the Petals Fall

This silent region of the mind is, also, a silence of the heart. For in the deeper and higher consciousness heart and mind are undivided.

Hugh l'Anson Fausset, *Fruits of Silence*

The deeper, therefore, we enter through the silence into communion with the divine, the more will our faith flower in knowledge. The silence will begin to speak.

Hugh l'Anson Fausset, *Fruits of Silence*

Until we have discovered the silence and what it enshrines, we cannot thus experience the deep related- ness of everything in life. Silence is the inner space which our faculties need if they are to function properly. One's words should be set in silence as objects are set in space.

Hugh l'Anson Fausset, *Fruits of Silence*

Understand the stillness. It is creative immobility where energies are concentrated. Think of it like still water beneath the rays of the sun. Give way to a process that is supremely natural, but unusual in the age you live in. Like the water you can move again when the stillness is over.

Margaret, Viscountess Long of Wraxall,
Let the Petals Fall

In the highest spiritual consciouness is a supreme stillness. You cannot accept this non-movement unless you have first experienced the turbulence of life on earth.

There is a purpose in sorrow for it illuminates joy.

Pure love is a state of oneness when all conflicting elements are stilled.

Margaret, Viscountess Long of Wraxall,
Let the Petals Fall

To recover his spiritual footing and thereby to find both inner freedom and real community with his fellows, man must regain contact ... with the silence within and beyond himself ... To regain the silence without which sound is a coarse affront to sensibility a man must turn inward in search of the world of being which underlies his outer existence, and in which consciousness originates and is unconditioned.

Hugh l'Anson Fausset, *Fruits of Silence*

Silence thyself and listen to the melody of the five trumpets coming down from Heaven – the heaven that is above the skies overhead. I laid the ears of my soul at the threshold of my heart and heard the shrouded mystery, but did not see anyone opening his mouth.

Hafiz Sahib,
(From Sant Kirpal Singh, *Jap Ji, the Message of Guru Nanak*)

A certain elder said: Apply yourself to silence, have no vain thoughts, and be intent on your meditation, whether you sit at prayer, or whether you rise up to work in the fear of God. If you do these things, you will not have to fear the attacks of the evil ones.

Thomas Merton, *The Wisdom of the Desert*

49

Silence thy thought and fix thy whole attention on thy Master whom thou dost not see, but whom thou feelest. Merge into one thy sense, if thou would'st be secure against the foe. 'Tis by that sense alone which lies concealed within the hollow of thy brain, that the steep path which leadeth to thy Master may be disclosed before thy Soul's dim eyes.

> H. P. Blavatsky, *The Voice of the Silence*

I do not connect love with emotion, but with a warmth and stillness, with happiness, with peace of mind, and givingness. There is a great happiness in giving from the heart.

> Olive C. B. Pixley, *The Armour of Light*

Grandfather, Great Spirit,
Today I sat for a short while in the thundering silence of
    your solitude.
And as I sat there, I saw a vision of how it was and how it
    is.
And how it was supposed to be, here in this part of your
    creation.
I thought about, and I saw with my limited vision,
The power and the sacredness and the beauty of your
    creation.
I give thanks for this new day.
Kitchi meegwetch!

> Art Solomon, Ojibway Indian Elder, *Silence*

Many are seeking but they alone find who remain in continual silence ... Every man who delights in a multitude of words, even though he says admirable things, is empty within. If you love truth, be a lover of silence. Silence like the sunlight will illuminate you in God and will deliver you from the phantoms of ignorance. Silence will invite you to God himself.

Isaak of Nineveh, Syrian Monk
(From Thomas Merton, *The Wisdom of the Desert*)

More than all things love silence; it brings you a fruit that tongue cannot describe. In the beginning we have to force ourselves to be silent. But then there is born something that draws us to silence. May God give you an experience of this 'Something' that is born of silence. If only you practise this, untold light will dawn on you in consequence ... After a while a certain sweetness is born in the heart of this exercise and the body is drawn almost by force to remain in silence.

Isaak of Nineveh, Syrian Monk
(From Thomas Merton, *The Wisdom of the Desert*)

The soul is immediately at one with God, when it is truly at peace in itself.

Julian of Norwich, *Revelation of Divine Love*

Oh Lord of the Eternities
Teach us of the mysteries,
Of the heights and depths
Of the Great Unknown.
Lead us down those trackless paths
Of thine eternal peace.
Feed our souls in the stillness,
That who-so-e'er comes near us,
Shall acknowledge Thy presence.

Sanskrit Prayer

The prayer of the heart introduces us into the deep interior silence so that we learn to experience its power. For that reason the prayer of the heart has to be always very simple, confined to the simplest of acts and often making use of no words and no thoughts at all.

Thomas Merton, *Contemplative Prayer*

Behold my beloved, I have shown you the power of silence, how thoroughly it heals and how fully pleasing it is to God. Wherefore I have written to you to show yourselves strong in this work you have undertaken, so that you may know that it is by silence that the saints grew, that it was because of silence that the power of God dwelt in them, because of silence that the mysteries of God were known to them.

Ammonas, Desert Father, Disciple of St Anthony
(From Thomas Merton, *Contemplative Prayer*)

Silence, for many people, allows the soul to grow and develop in its spiritual dimension. In fact, the more one finds the reality of silence, the more significant it becomes. While this in itself is a danger, the same is true of anything else we touch which has such real value.

Morton T. Kelsey, *The Other Side of Silence*

The Self reveals its essence only to him who applies himself to the Self. He who has not given up the ways of vice, who cannot control himself, who is not at peace within, whose mind is distracted, can never realize the Self, though full of all the learning in the world.

Katha Upanishad

If they ask you, 'What is the sign of your Father in you', say to them: 'It is a movement and a rest'.

The Gospel According to Thomas,
Nag Hammadi Gospels

Before and after each meal, express your gratitude verbally or silently to nature, the universe, or God who created the food and reflect on the health and happiness it is dedicated to achieving. This acknowledgment may take the form of grace, prayer, chanting, or a moment of silence.

Michio Kushi, *The Cancer Prevention Diet*

53

Grant, we beseech thee, merciful Lord to thy faithful people pardon and peace; that they may be cleansed from all their sins, and serve thee with a quiet mind

Collect. Twenty-first Sunday after Trinity,
Book of Common Prayer

What is important is to realise that there is a goal beyond this stillness, beyond the peace and relaxation or beyond the interest in extrasensory perception ... Each of the ways toward silence ... is an external device, a method meant to help the individual find a way to seek an individual experience of God through silence. Any of these practices can be helpful so long as one is fairly sure that this is a method that fills one's personal need, and then follows it consistently and sincerely toward the goal of being silent.

Morton T. Kelsey, *The Other Side of Silence*

His [Phineas Parkhurst Quimby's] method of contacting the Wisdom was based on a silent call or prayer. It was a method learned after much practice. When contact was made, it was accompanied by a sense of great force or power which was used in healing. This he came to call, 'the Power'.

Max Freedom Long, *The Secret Science Behind Miracles*

And the treatment of the soul, so he said, my wonderful friend, is by means of certain charms, and these charms are words of the right sort; by the use of such words is temperance engendered in our souls, and as soon as it is engendered and present we may easily secure health to the head, and to the rest of the body also. Now in teaching me the remedy and the charms he remarked: 'Let nobody persuade you to treat his head with this remedy, unless he has first submitted his soul for you to treat with the charm. For at present', he said, 'the cure of mankind is beset with error of certain doctors who attempt to practise the one method without the other.'

Socrates in Plato, *Charmides, 157*
[Affirmations for controlling the mind, c. 390 B.C.]

Many people find that it is easier to focus their attention on a sound than on their breathing. It is difficult to keep your mind from wandering when you repeat a sound mentally rather than verbally, but there is the advantage of being able to silently meditate anywhere.

Dean Ornish, *Stress, Diet and Your Heart,*
[Affirmations for controlling the mind, c. 1982]

I learned early on that 'stilling the mind' is a lot easier said than done ... Gradually we become our own observer. That part of ourselves that is observing is watching, not thinking – there is a part of us that is free from thought.

Penny Brohn, *The Bristol Programme*

... he who develops highly skilled patience will never expect anything from anyone, not because he is distrustful, but because he knows how to be at the centre and he IS the centre. So in order to achieve silence you would not chase the birds away because they make a noise. In order to be still you would not stop the movement of air or the rushing river, but accept them and you will yourself be aware of the silence. Just accept them as part of the establishment of silence.

Chogyam Trungpa, *Meditation In Action*

We have the antidote to our troubles available to us in the silence of our souls.

Unfortunately, experiencing anything approaching inner silence is usually rather a slow process and most people give it up too quickly.

Penny Brohn, *The Bristol Programme*

Let thy speech be better than silence – or be silent.

Dionysius, 367 B.C.
[also attributed to Pythagoras]

I have often repented of speaking, but rarely of holding my tongue.

See Publilius Syrus, Page 34   Zenocrates

56

This peace is embodied in the Soul of man; it is never dependent upon external condition; it exists as the gift of God in the midst of us. Our mistake has been in seeking peace from each other, in believing that others have the power to give or withhold peace, or in relying upon others for our harmony.

Joel S. Goldsmith, *The Art of Meditation*

Him have I known, the Great Spirit,
Him who is Light, who is beyond darkness.
To know Him, and Him alone, is to pass beyond death –
There is no other way.
He is the whole, other than He is naught,
Greater or smaller there is nothing other.
Still as a tree, unshaken in the heavens,
His living Being fills the Universe.

Svetasvatara Upanishad

Unquiet is the heart until it rests in Thee.

St Augustine, *Confessions*
Book 1: Chapter 1
(Trans. L. Watts)

If you would find an answer to every personal or world problem, practise the art of becoming very still within – as still and silent as the surface of a lake without a breath of wind to disturb it.

This lake represents your soul, and when it is still and you have developed the will of God within yourself, then you will see without distortion the reflection of truth on the waters of the lake which is your soul or 'psyche'. 'Be still, and know that I am God!' When man is alone with God, God speaks to him.

White Eagle, *Morning Light on the Spiritual Path*

Be still, my brother, be still and wait for the pointer to point the way. You cannot make a mistake if you do this, but it would be catastrophic if you rushed forward because you would certainly come up against a sharp instrument which would be painful. This is the cause of man's suffering. Until he learns to wait patiently on the Lord he will suffer.

White Eagle, *The Quiet Mind*

White Eagle says: 'In order to receive impressions from the inner or soul world, it is of the utmost importance that the activity of the brain should be stilled. You cannot receive impressions from the soul world if the brain is too active. We take an illustration for you of a pool of clear water. If the water is ruffled then the impressions made on that water become distorted, but if that pool is absolutely still it can reflect perfectly. We use this illustration because water is associated with the soul, with the psyche.'

Grace Cooke, *The Jewel in the Lotus*

58

Sometimes the voice comes from the inner world at the etheric level, when it is called the 'direct voice', or 'direct hearing', but this is not the way one hears in meditation. It is an inner voice, the voice of the silence, that is heard in deep meditation, which is not the same as a semi-physical voice which comes through the psychic materialisation of the dense etheric atoms.

Grace Cooke, *The Jewel in the Lotus*

We have to learn how to acquire and maintain a stillness – peace and poise within . . .

When you have learnt the power of silence, the quietude of spirit, you will be amazed to discover your spiritual hearing has become enhanced. You will find there is a connection between the throat centre and hearing . . .

Much noise and idle speech is harmful. Noise dissipates, silence strengthens power. And these things bring to you: Spiritual Peace.

White Eagle, *Spiritual Unfoldment*, Vol. 1 (1942)

Cosmic truths should never be spoken or written, but must come to the soul in the silence of its own temple. Do you understand? The inner secrets of life are yours at your initiation. Initiation means an expansion of consciousness; and at these times, a great light illumines the understanding, and the soul is changed.

White Eagle, *Spiritual Unfoldment*, Vol. 2 (1943)

To hear your true note or tone, however, you must learn to find the silence. To find your note or tone sounded on any instrument will be most difficult, although you may go near to it. If all souls were true to their intuition, or voice of their spirit, rapid progress would be made, but most people are too noisy themselves or too busy with others to listen-in to the silence.

White Eagle, *Spiritual Unfoldment*, Vol. 3 (1944)

How shall we listen-in to that higher mind? The old idea of making yourself passive, negative, nebulous, before entering into the silence is a great waste of time ... We have told you to make yourself quiet, tranquil, to be still – but to attain and to maintain this stillness under the direction of the spirit, which is vastly different from becoming vaguely dreamy and nebulous. From this stillness within, you will direct your journey with yourself so firmly in hand that you forbid intrusion by the outer, daily mind upon your meditation; you will control yourself, not by knitting your brow and making a mighty effort with the brain, but by quiet and steady exercise of will by the heart-centre. Holding yourself poised, you will meet and know God.

White Eagle, *Spiritual Unfoldment*, Vol 3 (1944)

Let us make this quite clear. The cultivation of silence in the breast, the cultivation of response to the inner voice, will lead the aspirant to the reception of the clear Voice of the Master, whose command he awaits.

White Eagle, *Spiritual Unfoldment*, Vol 4 (1944)

Man has to learn to seek first the kingdom of heaven, the place of stillness and quiet at the highest level of which he is capable, and then the heavenly influences can pour into him, recreate him and use him for the salvation of mankind.

White Eagle, *The Quiet Mind*

The wise man learns so much through silence. How wise is he who has learnt to discriminate between what to say, and what to leave unsaid! Wise also is he who can listen to the spoken word and understand the language of the spirit behind.

White Eagle, *The Gentle Brother*

You think of peace as meaning goodwill towards each other, goodwill among the nations, the laying down of arms. But peace is far more than this; it can only be understood and realised within your heart. It lies beneath all the turmoil and noise and clamour of the world, beneath feeling, beneath thought. It is found in the deep, deep silence and stillness of the soul. It is spirit; in other words, it is God, your creator.

White Eagle, *The Gentle Brother*

... the need is to slow down the scurrying, bustling self-absorbed outer man, so that its demands gradually drop away. Successful reception is not achieved by making the mind a blank, as so often advised, which usually merely produces tension, but by stilling the outer mind so that the very much quieter voice of the inner self can commence to be heard. Meditation is peaceful. Peace in turn deepens vision and helps to keep it steady. Meditation is a process of a giving and receiving freely within the soul; it is everything the market place is not.

Paul Beard, *Hidden Man*

The early stages of teaching present what can easily be grasped; it is for immediate use. The inner part remains, suspended, inaudible, until pupils one by one can and do enter into that inner silence where it can be received. This calls for growth in serenity, a growth usually needing very persevering cultivation. It will necessarily come and go in the early stages. For even when serenity is well established, much of the meaning still remains in the invisible – contained in the mind of the teacher as he watches over his flock – and cannot be commanded by the most attentive ear. It has to be awaited.

Paul Beard, *Hidden Man*

When he [the student] truly faces his own imperfections, a deep peace gradually arises. This peace is one of the keys which guides seek to impart. It can be felt both in their words and in their presence. It is perhaps their most valuable gift to us.

Paul Beard, *Hidden Man*

62

There is only one sure way of entering the kingdom of heaven, and this is through the heart, through love, through becoming at-one with the God Who dwells in the silence within the heart.

White Eagle, *The Brotherhood Teaching*

So people who look at life from their deep silent centre know that the lighted hours and the dark hours are determined by our turning. When we turn our attention to the soul's prompting, there is a clear light to see by; when we shun or hide from the light, there is darkness.

Margaret Rompage, *The Sun Path*

Silence, and a far sounding bell.
No words, which broken winged presume,
Themselves of caged flight, to tell
The beyond of our imaginings.
Two slow-descending points illumine
The graven stillness.

Christmas Humphreys, 'Zen-Do',
From: *Both Sides of The Circle*

With the attainment of his majority man is now passing beyond the stage when the services of a personal mediator are necessary to his spiritual development. When his mind assumes its true function he will understand that its purpose is to serve as a vehicle through which God is made manifest on earth. In the hidden depths of his own nature he will discover the power to do for himself all that he has depended upon others to do for him. He will learn how to heal himself, govern himself, understand himself and so discover for himself the path that leads to the Kingdom of Heaven within his own heart.

Vera W. Reid, *Towards Aquarius*

In tranquillity the mind perceives its inner stillness; contemplate that stillness that you may attain perception of the all-pervading void.

John Blofeld, *Beyond the Gods*

But the Lord is in his holy temple; let all the earth keep silence before him.

Habakkuk 2:20

But for those first affections,
Those shadowy recollections,
Which, be they what they may,
Are yet the fountain-light of all our day,
Are yet a master light of all our seeing;
Uphold us, cherish, and have power to make
Our noisy years seem moments in the being
Of the eternal silence: truths that wake,
To perish never . . .

Wordsworth, *Intimations of Immortality*

Try to understand – it is so simple and yet so all-inclusive. If you would progress to the heart of the mysteries of the cosmos, your way lies always through meditation upon and realisation of the still small voice, the God within. All the wonderful mysteries of Atlantis, Persia, Egypt, China are secreted within your heart, dormant, yet ineffaceable. This is why you must learn to be still . . .

A paradox. We first tell you to be still, and then to savour life to its fullest! Yet to know God you must learn to live more abundantly. For who can learn of God if he remains isolated from his kind?

White Eagle, *Spiritual Unfoldment*, Vol. 1 (1942)

The symbol of Christ is the Cross of sacrifice. The symbol of the Buddha is the Lotus Flower, representative of stillness and renunciation of outer world claims.

White Eagle, *The Brotherhood Teaching*

Silently comes the Kingdom. No man can judge when It enters the heart of man, only in results. Listen quietly. Sometimes you may get no message. Meet this all the same. You will absorb an atmosphere. Cultivate silence. 'God speaks in silences'. A silence, a soft wind. Each can be a message to convey My meaning to the heart, though by no voice, or even, word.

Two Listeners, *God Calling* (ed. A. J. Russell)

With us the words we do not speak become prayers. There lies our strength, and we can do no good except through this wonderful medium of silence. We speak to God of those to whom our lips are closed. We must ask God for the grace to find ourselves, instead of running away from ourselves – these are mere figures of speech. What they signify, and the truth deeper than themselves in which they find their true interpretation, is this. There is within us the object of our aspirations.

A Carthusian, *They Speak by Silences*

Silence. Be silent before Me. Seek to know and then to do My will in all things.

Two Listeners, *God Calling* (ed. A. J. Russell)

Endeavour to find yourself, the real 'I' beneath the outer coats of flesh and mind which obscure it. To do this try to think in terms of three; first, think of the ordinary person that you are in daily life; think about the soul, known only to yourself (or so you think); and thirdly, try to find the place of stillness and quiet at the centre of your being, the real 'I'.

White Eagle, *Golden Harvest*

So silently I teach, and that silent teaching depends upon your approach. Let every discipline, every joy, every difficulty, every fresh interest serve to draw you nearer, serve to render you more receptive to My word, serve to make you more sensitive, more spiritually aware.

Two Listeners, *God at Eventide*, (ed. A. J. Russell)

Silence is in truth the attribute of God, and those who seek him from that side learn that meditation is not the dream but the reality of life; not its illusion, but its truth; not its weakness, but its strength.

James Martineau
(From E. Hermann, *Creative Prayer*)

Silence is the nutriment of devotion.

Thomas à Kempis, *The Imitation of Christ*

Space, the bound of a solid –
Silence, then, the form of a Melody.
. . . Man, on his way to silence, stops to hear and see.
Alice Meynell, *To Silence*

Have you not heard His silent steps?
Rabindranath Tagore

. . . it is the silent effortless radiance of deep being which ensures the most powerful action at a distance. This has proved itself true thousands of times, in space as well as time.
Hermann Keyserling, *From Suffering to Fulfilment*

To achieve and maintain the inner silence is a difficult task which calls for persistence and a firm determination; it is a sustained act of will. Our psychological mechanism is not accustomed to such discipline, it resents it and tries in every way to shake it off . . .

There are several techniques we can use; one is to repeat over and over a phrase or word; another is to evoke an image and keep it clear and steady at the centre of consciousness. The best words and images for this purpose are those which suggest a state of calm, of peace, of silence. An effective phrase for example (from a Hymn used in the Greek Mysteries) is: 'Be silent, that a new melody may come to me'. Images such as the following are helpful in stilling the mind: a quiet lake reflecting the blue of the sky; a majestic mountain peak; the starry sky in the stillness of night.

Sundial House, *Meditation for the New Age*

Meditation is silent and unuttered prayer, or, as Plato expressed it, 'the ardent turning of the soul towards the divine; not to ask any particular good (as is the common meaning of prayer), but for good itself – for the universal Supreme Good' of which we are a part on earth, and out of which we have all emerged. Therefore, adds Plato, 'remain silent in the presence of the divine ones, till they remove the clouds from thy eyes and enable thee to see by the light which issues from themselves, not what appears as good to thee, but what is intrinsically good.'

H. P. Blavatsky, *The Key to Theosophy*
[See also: *Isis Unveiled*, Vol. I]

As we give out, so does the whole man – physically and mentally – become depleted, yet in entering into the silence, entering into the silence in meditation, with a clean hand, a clean body, a clean mind, we may receive that strength and power that fits each individual, each soul, for a greater activity in this material world.

Edgar Cayce, *Reading* 281:13

The word mystical derives from the Greek mystos, 'keeping silence'. Mystical experience reveals pheno-mena that are usually silent and inexplicable. This extended consciousness, this whole-knowing, transcends our limited powers of description. Sensation, perception, and intuition seem to merge to create something that is none of these.

Marilyn Ferguson, *The Aquarian Conspiracy*
(Greek: Musterion. Muo: close lips or eyes.
Oxford Dictionary)

If you inhibit thought (and persevere) you come at length to a region of consciousness below thought ... and a realization of an altogether vaster self than that to which we are accustomed. And since the ordinary conscious-ness, with which we are concerned in ordinary life, is before all things founded on the little local self ... it follows that to pass out of that is to die to the ordinary self and the ordinary world.

It is to die in the ordinary sense, but in another, it is to wake up and find that the 'I', one's real, most intimate self, pervades the universe and all other beings.

So great, so splendid, is this experience, that it may be said that all minor questions and doubts fall away in the face of it; and certain it is that in thousands and thousands of cases, the fact of its having come even once to an individual has completely revolutionized his subsequent life and outlook on the world.

Edward Carpenter, *The Drama of Love and Death*

There are two ways of contemplation of Brahman: in sound and in silence. By sound we go to silence. The sound of Brahman is OM. With OM we go the End: the silence of Brahman. The End is immortality, union and peace. Even as a spider reaches the liberty of space by means of its own thread, the man of contemplation by means of OM reaches freedom.

Maitri Upanishad, 6:22

In order to reach the Highest, consider in adoration the sound and the silence of Brahman. For it has been said: God is sound and silence. His name is OM. Attain therefore contemplation in silence on Him.

Maitri Upanishad, 6:23

The mind of man is of two kinds, pure and impure: impure when in the bondage of desire, pure when free from desire.

When the mind is silent, beyond weakness or non-concentration, then it can enter into a world which is beyond the mind: the Highest End. The mind should be kept in the heart as long as it has not reached the Highest End. This is wisdom, and this is liberation. Everything else is only words.

Maitri Upanishad, 6:24

There are two birds, sweet friends, who dwell on the self-same tree. The one eats the fruits thereof, and the other looks on in silence. The first is the human soul who, resting on that tree, though active, feels sad in his unwisdom. But on beholding the power and glory of the higher Spirit, he becomes free from sorrow.

Mundaka Upanishad, Part 3, Ch 1 and
Svetasvara Upanishad, Part 4

When the five senses and the mind are still, and reason itself rests in silence, then begins the Path supreme. This calm steadiness of the senses is called Yoga. Then one should become watchful, because Yoga comes and goes. Words and thoughts cannot reach him and he cannot be seen by the eye. How can he then be perceived except by him who says 'He is'? In the faith of 'He is' his existence must be perceived, and he must be perceived in his essence. When he is perceived as 'He is', then shines forth the revelation of his essence.

Katha Upanishad, Part 6

As the bird-watcher watches the bird without interference and in silence so we have to find a way to gain direct and impartial insight into our own mechanisms . . .

Initially, this requires direct self-acquired and impartial knowledge of the nature of the endlessly chattering mind and the emotional currents that accompany it and eventually a recognition of the fact that the superficial mind and intellect have no power to grasp the deeper causes that lie under the surface. Then, with the stilling of this monkey stung by a scorpion, as it has been described, and the cultivation of alert and total attention, real answers may begin to appear. Answers from a new dimension which will change the whole life and make it meaningful and intelligent.

Carl Upton, Holism in Medicine, *Psionic Journal*, 1985

In contemplating the Supreme Being it is most fitting to be silent, aware that while the human mind is an instrument of value in its proper sphere, it is wholly incapable of grasping the highest reality, that quality of consciousness which we have labelled Spirit. If however we feel driven to philosophise, we can do no other than take the highest values we know, Love, Truth, Beauty, Wisdom, etc., and regard the Supreme Being as the source and sustainer of these values.

Raynor Johnson, *The Light and the Gate*

Fear in some form or another is the root from which grows so much evil. The real mystic is above and beyond all fear, resting within the deep peace of God. But he does not reach that position in most cases unless he has been through much conflict, and experienced many trials.

Ambrose Pratt
(From Raynor Johnson, *The Light and the Gate*)

Never wish to shine, or to appear clever; have no desire to speak. It is well to speak little; better still to say nothing, unless you are quite sure that what you say is true, kind and helpful. Before speaking think carefully whether what you are going to say has those three qualities; if it has not, do not say it.

It is well to get used even now to thinking carefully before speaking; for when you reach Initiation you must watch every word, lest you should tell what must not be told ... One statement of the Qualifications [for the spiritual Path] gives them thus: to know, to dare, to will, and to be silent; and the last of the four is the hardest of them all.

Alcyone, *At the Feet of the Master*

Know then, that he who would know God must of necessity withdraw from the hurry of material life and listen to Him in the hurricane, in the raging of the sea, in the cry of humanity, in the innumerable sounds all about him, for there God is; only He must be singled out in the silence of celestial sounds, in silence of the soul's ecstasy, in the great spiritual moments of the heart's devotion.

Mabel Beatty, *Man Made Perfect*

Give me my scallop shell of quiet,
My staff of faith to walk upon,
My scrip of joy, immortal diet,
My bottle of salvation,
My gown of Glory, hope's true gage,
And thus I'll take my pilgrimage.
Sir Walter Raleigh, *The Passionate Man's Pilgrimage*

. . . There is no stone on earth to which I do not respond. They speak to me and I understand their language. When a sacred stillness pervades me and my soul becomes a cathedral, where the light of the spirit shines within, then my inner amethysts flash in the mysterious depths of my being and I become aware that purple is the colour of that spiritual light that heals.

Mellie Uyldert, *The Magic of Precious Stones*

There are few people today who are able to lead a leisurely life. The solution therefore lies in not only curtailing over-activity whenever possible, but changing one's attitude, learning to find inner stillness even in the midst of activity, and then working from that point. In the words of an eastern scripture –

'Both action and inaction may find room in thee; thy body agitated, thy mind tranquil, thy soul limpid as a mountain lake.'

Sundial House, *Meditation for the New Age*

'Though sendest forth the word, and the earth is flooded with silence, O thou only One,
Who didst dwell in heaven before ever the earth and the mountains came into existence.'

Litany to the Sun God, *Egyptian Book of the Dead*

The spirit of man loves purity, but his mind disturbs it. The mind of man loves stillness, but his desires draw it away. If he could always send his desires away, his mind would of itself become still. Let his mind be made clean, and his spirit of itself will become pure.

Khing Kang King, *The Classic of Purity, 3*

There is a direct hot line like the one from America to Moscow that goes from the hypothalamus to the pituitary gland . . . So that means every thought you have can also affect your neuro-endocrine balance . . .

. . . the most important thing is to reduce the sensory input into the computer area, or black box area, of the brain; and if you do this the brain becomes aware of other sorts of information. And I mean specifically intuitive information . . .

Ann Woolley-Hart, 'Beyond Biofeedback'
Radionic Journal, December 1979

Baron von Hugel expresses a tradition that goes back to Origen when he says, 'Man is what he does with his silence'. There is a terror in silence if one is only conscious of being an isolated individual, because man is made for fellowship, to be part of a family. Although speech is a necessary means of communication, there is a whole realm of human – as well as spirital – exploration in which silence can be the medium of a positive exchange of communication. Why? For one thing, in silence there is not the same opportunity for our own egoism – the false I – to cover up a frightening emptiness.

Mother Mary Clare, *Silence and Prayer*

Our first step in meditative silence is to forget completely the physical mechanism. The body must be at ease, relaxed, comfortable.

The second step is a little more difficult for most of us. It is the control, or perhaps a better word would be supersedence, of the mental process. We are working for a state of consciousness which is beyond reason and above mental activity, as we know it in the form of thought. We want to rise above the mental processes far enough so that thoughts do not intrude upon the silence which we seek ... In meditation we are re-forming, rebuilding and remaking. As we are reborn into the world of the spirit we find we have many habits which belong to the world of the material. To accomplish the things we wish to accomplish, and reach the place we wish to attain, it is necessary for us to build new habits and replace old ones until we establish ourselves firmly in the full consciouness of this reality which is beyond the senses.

Rebecca Beard, *Everyman's Search*

The condition, then, for clear and perfect reception is one of stillness of mind and silence; not only on the outer plane but deep, deep, deep within the inner world, the inner place. Beyond all conflicting vibrations is the silence; and that silence is God. God is behind all form, all activity, all manifestation.

White Eagle, *Sunrise*

Meditation in any of its forms is a wonderful way to quiet the mind and allow your own 'knowingness' to come to the surface. I usually just sit with my eyes closed and say, 'What is it I need to know?' and then wait quietly for an answer. If the answer comes, fine; if it doesn't fine. It will come another day.

Louise L. Hay, *You Can Heal Your Life*

If we really want to pray we must first learn to listen, for in the silence of the heart God speaks. And to be able to see that silence, to be able to hear God, we need a clean heart, for a clean heart can see God, can hear God, can listen to God ... When it is difficult to pray, we must help ourselves do so. The first means to use is silence, for souls of prayer are souls of great silence. We cannot put ourselves directly in the presence of God if we do not practise internal and external silence ... God is the friend of silence.

Mother Teresa of Calcutta, *In the Silence of The Heart*

Be very still and quiet, but also have the joy of the spirit singing within you and laughter in your face. The Elder Brethren have a lively sense of humour, and love laughter.

White Eagle, *Sunrise*

The more we receive in silent prayer, the more we can give in our active life . . .

Silence gives us a new outlook on everything . . .

We need silence to be able to touch souls. The essential thing is not what we say but what God says to us and through us . . .

Interior silence is very difficult but we must make the effort. In silence we will find new energy and true unity. The energy of God will be ours to do all things well.

Mother Teresa of Calcutta, *In the Silence of The Heart*

If you can accept God as 'the One who listens', then talking to Him about yourself (and everything and everyone in your life) makes sense. But it also makes sense to learn how to listen to Him without just chattering on. This learning is not all that easy, because we need to still ourselves; and we do not listen with the physical ear, but somehow in a way unknown, we become aware of the still small voice, which 'speaks' to our own stillness . . . the voice of 'the One who listens'. Once you know or experience this, you listen as He listens – and it spreads to everything and continues always all the time, and this is when we can say that silence speaks to silence.

Michael Hollings and Etta Gullick, *The One Who Listens*

... the still, small voice is never heard in the thunder or the whirlwind, but only in the silence. The higher contacts give a sense of power, of protection, of peace; they do not speak with voices.

Dion Fortune, *Practical Occultism in Daily Life*

... psychiatrists know well the truth of the old proverbs 'Shallow brooks are noisy' and 'Still waters run deep'.

M. Scott Peck, *The Road Less Travelled*

Meditate awhile quietly on the *meaning* of:

Here and now I draw from the fountain of Life to manifest my existence in God. From the wellspring of Love so that I reflect His Love in fellowship and service to others.

From the source of Wisdom in order to understand the purpose of my life and to fulfil it.

The time will come both for you and for me, when as a result, a deep silence will descend upon us, a silent stillness filled with the love of God. And out of the silence a still small voice will make itself heard and the answer we seek will be both yours and mine.

When this happens how wonderful it will be to go our ways rejoicing and be at peace.

Wellesley Tudor Pole, *The Silent Road*

Blessed are they who serve,
Blessed are they who love.
Blessed are they who are wise, with the wisdom of love.
Blessed are they who are silent.
Blessed are they whose feet have been set upon the path
leading up to the mountains of spiritual aspiration, to
the Golden City.
For in that City they will find their heart's desire.

Author Unknown

It becomes possible to await the unfolding of events
without the customary anxious expectancy, and thereby
to savour impressions of the present moment which are
ignored in the feverish pursuit of desire.

This is patience, – an impersonal state quite different
from resignation, having the quality of stillness.

There is an apt poem which runs:

> 'Where shall wisdom be found?
> Be still and know.
> Seek the strength of no desire.'

(From 'The Flame in the Heart', by C. E. Bignall)
J. H. Reyner, *A Philosophy of Delight*

Through meditation and quiet contemplation the outer layers of the mind and emotion are gradually laid aside and man rests in the innermost place of stillness where the jewel of truth lies, the jewel within the lotus of his heart. This is the light that lighteth every man, the Christ the Son of God in him. Search for it, my brethren, but not with a great deal of noise and talk; just quietly keep on keeping on, searching in the stillness of your own innermost being. The mind must be stilled, and the spirit must become aware, must become conscious of its being. Then the soul of man becomes illumined with the divine spirit and consciousness expands into the worlds of beauty and truth which bring peace and joy to the human soul.

White Eagle, *The Still Voice*

There is one direction in particular where modern civilisation has fallen into grievous error. The value of silence and the training of the mind to become still and receptive has ceased to be recognised and practised. We educate our children almost entirely through the use of noise. They are taught to focus their attention upon what they hear and see . . . The immense importance of silence as an integral part of education is rarely recognised. Training in the stilling of the mind, in thought control, is never given and the results are serious. The practice of silence can become a healing and educative agency, and it is time that this truth should be recognised and made available, both for children and adults alike.

Wellesley Tudor Pole, *The Silent Road*

Stillness is the road. The still mind does not seek or ask. It is already there, simultaneously at the beginning and the end. It looks and sees what it is.

Barry Long, *Meditation, A Foundation Course*

A lesson we find hard to learn, a lesson all must heed. Peace comes to those who are at peace within. Such inner peace is worth a thousand victories on the outer battlefields of life. Be quiet! Listen for that inner voice! The still, small voice – obey it! Never act without its mandate first. Purify the sanctuary within your soul, that the Christ may walk therein.

Wellesley Tudor Pole, *The Silent Road*

Why should we not each have a 'King's House' within the central desert of our being; a sanctuary where we could retire from storm and stress, where in the central stillness we could gain poise and strength and renew our faith? ... I am still learning the lesson that is eternally waiting within the King's Chamber of the Great Pyramid to teach itself unto the minds of men: Silence, Stillness, Sanctuary; then the Summit.

From the silence of time, time's silence borrow.
In the heart of today is the Word of tomorrow.
The Builders of Joy are the children of sorrow.

(Triad by William Sharp)

Wellesley Tudor Pole, *The Silent Road*

Silence is power, for when we reach the place of silence in mind, we have reached the place of power – the place where all is one, the one power – God. 'Be still and know that I am God'. Diffused power is noise. Concentrated power is silence. When through concentration (driving to a center), we have brought all our force into one point of force, we have contacted God in silence, we are one with Him and hence with all power. This is the heritage of man. 'I and the Father are one.' . . . Only as we turn from the without to the silence of the within, can we hope to make conscious union with God.

Baird T. Spalding, *Life and Teaching of the Masters of the Far East*, Vol. 1

Those who approach the Lord should make their prayer in a state of quietness, of peace and great tranquillity without uneasy and confused cries but by applying their attention to the Lord by the effort of the heart and the soberness of their thoughts.

Pseudo Macarius, *Sixth Homily* [4th to 5th Century]

Her [Frances Banks] belief was that, through meditation, through retiring into the deep centre of oneself and finding the place of silence of the soul, communion could be established with advanced souls; higher beings, great ones whom we call Saints. This is the true communion of Saints; a One-ness with the Divine Company of Heaven, resulting in a new intuitive perception of unity and inspiration for radiant living.

Helen Greaves, *Testimony of Light*

Profound and tender souls need silence and peace to spring into manifestation.

Edouard Schuré, *Jesus, the Last Great Initiate*

Let my thoughts be silent that I may feel Thee.

Helen Boddington, *Little Steps in the Way of Silence*

... 'Silence is one of the greatest helps in Soul-growth', and should therefore be cultivated by the aspirant in his home, his personal demeanour, his walk, his habits, and paradoxical as it seems even in his speech ... we can *and must* at least cultivate the virtue of silence in ourselves or our own soul-growth will be very small.

Max Heindel, *Christian Mysticism*

Silence is a healing for all ailments. Silence is good for the wise; how much more for the foolish. All my days I have grown up amongst the wise, and I have found naught of better service than silence.

Hebrew Proverb

What sleep does for our body and nervous system, silence does for our mind and spirit.

Swami Paramanda, *Silence as Yoga*

'In the midst of Silence there was spoken within me a secret word.' 'But sir, where is the Silence and where is the place where the word is spoken?' – As I said . . . it is in the purest thing that the soul is capable of, in the noblest part, the ground – indeed, in the very essence of the soul which is the soul's most secret part.

Meister Eckhart, *Sermons and Treatises*, Vol. 1

There are two ways to practise silence. One is through absence of thought. The other through fullness of thought. The second is productive of great strength . . . When . . . we are able to fill the mind with one dynamic thought, not only does it fortify us against outer and inner dangers, but of itself will empty the mind of all alien thoughts . . . In *Sattwa* we have the positive silence; in *Tamas*, the negative. The two kinds may seem to resemble each other outwardly. One overpowered by dullness may appear tranquil; but it is a very different condition from the serene stillness of *Sattwa*, where all the faculties are wide awake and full of light.

Swami Paramanda, *Silence as Yoga*

Lady and the unicorn: The relationship between the Feminine soul, or Anima, and the spirit or Self. As the story goes, the soul cannot capture the essence of life, or realize its inner unity, by running hectically from activity to activity, but only by sitting down quietly, which is how the lady Anima catches the unicorn. This refers to what can only be achieved by passiveness, openness, receptivity in the inner work.

Tom Chetwynd, *A Dictionary of Symbols*

Whenever we follow our higher instincts, instead of our lower, we humanize the animal in us and the noisier, more excitable part of our nature is quieted. The idea of silence is not merely avoiding action; it is bringing all our scattered and undisciplined forces wholly under control.

Swami Paramanda, *Silence as Yoga*

Although sincerity is of utmost importance, at times silence is the only medicine that can cure this world of ignorance. Speak the truth when it is inspiring, encouraging, illuminating, and fruitful. But when the truth will create measureless misunderstanding and untold suffering, silence is by far the best truth.

Sri Chinmoy, *Silence Invites No Problems*
(A story told to the United Nations Meditation Group)

The practice of silence has to do with every part of our system. There is a silence of the body, a silence of the mind and a silence of the heart. Until all these are tranquillized, we cannot know what true silence is ... The sages declare that each one can make for himself an inner island, where no storm can overwhelm. This is the purpose of all spiritual practice.

Swami Paramanda, *Silence as Yoga*

Man always recovers from the effect of his sense-life when he turns his mind inward to the Father's House. There is a place within the depth of man's consciousness that is the Father's House. It is that which is spoken of by the Psalmist when he said, 'He that dwelleth in the secret place of the Most High shall abide under the shadow of the Almighty'.

The world of the senses is a noisy place. The world of the Spirit is the place of peace. The world of the senses tears one to pieces. The world of the Spirit heals and integrates him.

It is a man's privilege to close his ears to the raucous voices of the world of the senses, and penetrate deeper and deeper into the world of Reality which lies within . . . the few make their way into the heart of Reality, where the aches, pains, and sickness of life cannot send up their discordant voices. These are they who dwell in the secret place of the Most High . . . Dwell deep, my soul, dwell deep. This is the secret of peace.

Frederick Bailes, *Your Mind Can Heal You*

. . . In order to maintain an attitude of relaxation and quietness – and one that is not purely passive – the will is still required, to act, metaphorically, as the watchman at the door of consciousness to exclude intruders.

Roberto Assagioli, *Psychosynthesis*

Absolute stillness for as long as possible is best of all for you. You cannot exchange this state for any other without harm. That is certain.

Meister Eckhart, *Sermons and Treatises*, Vol 1

'... for the self individualization of the soul it is necessary to be much alone, because in this silence and aloneness, the soul gradually becomes self-individualized, it is able to hold converse with the Father in Heaven ... These periods of quietness can take place at any time, it matters not whether it is morning, noon or evening. The Conscious mind is stilled, and the Super-conscious mind blends with the Sub-conscious mind, making you a different person, because you have put away earthly things and are companioned by Angels.'

'I-Em-Hotep' through Mrs K. Barkel,
The Hermetic Philosophy

If Jesus is to speak in the soul, she must be all alone, and she has to be quiet herself to hear what he says.

Meister Eckhart, *Sermons and Treatises*, Vol. 1

Men seek retirement in country house, on shore or hill; and you too know full well what that yearning means. Surely a very simple wish; for at what hour you will, you can retire into yourself. Nowhere can man find retirement more peaceful and untroubled than in his own soul; specially he who hath such stores within, that at a glance he straightway finds himself lapped in ease; meaning by ease good order in the soul, this and nothing else. Ever and anon grant yourself this retirement, and so renew yourself. Have at command thoughts, brief and elemental, yet effectual to shut out the court and all its ways, and send you back unchafing to the tasks to which you must return.

Marcus Aurelius Antoninus, *To Himself*

For silence is not God, nor speaking; fasting is not God, nor eating; solitude is not God, nor company; nor any other pair of opposites. He is hidden between them, and cannot be found by anything your soul does, but only by the love of your heart. He cannot be known by reason, he cannot be thought, caught, or sought by understanding. But he can be loved and chosen by the true, loving will of your heart. Then choose him, and you will speak by your silence, and there will be silence in your speech, you will be fasting while you eat, and eating when you fast . . .

The Anonymous Author of 'The Cloud of Unknowing',
A Study of Wisdom

He [Pythagoras] spoke many precepts regarding silence, including this: 'Of all forms of continence, the bridling of the tongue is the most difficult'. The familiar testimony to the need for aloneness is in the admonition: 'Leave the public roads, and walk in unfrequented paths.'

Sheldon Cheney, *Men Who Have Walked with God*

And we began to say: If to any the tumult of the flesh were hushed; hushed the images of earth, of waters and of air; hushed also the poles of heaven; yea, were the very soul to be hushed to herself, and by not thinking on self to surmount self; hushed all dreams and imaginary revelations, every tongue and every sign; if all transitory things were hushed utterly, – for to him that heareth they do all speak, saying 'we made not ourselves, but He made us, who abideth for ever' – if, when their speech had gone out they should suddenly hold their peace, and to the ear which they had aroused to their Maker, He himself should speak, alone, not by them but by himself, so that we should hear his word . . .

St Augustine, *Confessions*, IX, 10

To realise the difference between reflective and receptive meditation it is useful to consider the mind as an 'inner eye', which in a certain respect it truly is . . . in receptive meditation we direct the mind's eye 'upwards' and try to discern what is 'above', on a higher level than that on which we are aware . . . This stage should be defined carefully, because there are various kinds of silence. The safe and true kind needed is a *positive* silence, that is, the maintaining of a positive inner stillness for the desired period, in which we eliminate as much as possible of all spontaneous activity of the mind.

This phase of silence is a necessary condition for receiving and registering higher influences . . .

To achieve and maintain the inner silence is a difficult task which calls for persistence and a firm determination; it is a sustained act of the will. Our psychological mechanism is not accustomed to such discipline, it resents it and tries in every way to shake it off . . .

There are several techniques we can use, one is to repeat over and over a phrase or word; another is to evoke an image and keep it clear and steady at the centre of consciousness. The best words and images for this purpose are those which suggest a state of calm, of peace, of silence.

Sundial House, *Meditation for the New Age*

The mind controls or influences the immune system right down to cellular level. We can use this knowledge to speed healing, to reverse pathology, and to prevent ill-health if we can learn to harness the power present in all of us. This is best achieved by use of guided imagery or visualisation.

In order to use visualisation to achieve therapeutic healing, or prevention, it is necessary to be able to relax and then to learn to focus the mind on one idea, sound or image. Only when the body is physically relaxed and the mind stilled from the chatter which usually clutters its activities, can the full benefits of visualisation be realised.

> Leon Chaitow, 'Not All In The Mind but . . .'
> *Here's Health*, February 1989

People who regularly elicit the Relaxation Response become more spiritual . . . Dr Cass and other of his colleagues have been able to define and work out a measure of spirituality which isn't: 'Do you believe in God?' because most people will respond, either through belief, or superstition, that they do, but rather: 'Have you experienced the Presence of something beyond you?' . . . People regularly eliciting the Relaxation Response, be it through a religious mode or a secular mode, *have* the experience that there is something beyond them and they become more spiritual, and furthermore, it is appearing in very preliminary studies, that to the extent that this occurs, many people get better.

Herbert Benson, Wrekin Trust and Confederation of Healing Organisations Conference 1988 (Recorded Talk)

Excitement is alien to the spiritual life.

Arthur E. Powell, *The Astral Body*

While we live we shall approach nearest to intuitive knowledge if we hold no communion with the body, except what absolute necessity requires, not suffer ourselves to be pervaded by its nature, but purify ourselves from it until God himself shall release us.

Socrates in Plato, *Phaedo*

... 'peak experience' can occur at any time and in any place when the busy-ness of the mind is stilled for an instant and the individual *perceives* in quietness and silence.

Is this difficult? Yes, because it is too simple, and our lives are usually lived in action and complexity. What we need is not to do but to stop doing, and find the wonders of the quiet mind. Then ... we shall hear the 'Voice of the Silence', which is that of the gods or angels among whom we dwell.

Laurence J. Bendit, *The Mysteries Today*

The true condition of quiet, according to the great mystics, is at once active and passive: it is pure surrender, but a surrender which is not limp self-abandonment, but rather the free and constantly renewed self-giving and self-emptying of a burning love. The departmental intellect is silenced, but the totality of character is flung open to the influence of the Real.

... though the psychological state which contemplatives call the prayer of quiet is a common condition of mystical attainment, it is not by itself mystical at all. It is a state of preparation: a way of opening the door. That which comes in when the door is opened will be that which we truly and passionately desire. The will makes plain the way: the heart – the whole man – conditions the guest.

Evelyn Underhill, *Mysticism*

Michael is a silent Spirit – silent and taciturn. The other ruling Archangels are talkative Spirits – in a spiritual sense, of course; but Michael is taciturn. He is a Spirit who speaks very little ... We only come to Michael when we get through the words to real inner experiences of the spirit when we do not hang on the words, but arrive at real inner experiences of the spirit.

This is the very essence, the secret of modern Initiation: to get beyond the words to a living experience of the spiritual.

Rudolf Steiner,
The Festivals and their Meaning: Michaelmas

A wise old owl lived in an oak.
The more he saw the less he spoke.
The less he spoke the more he heard.
Why can't we be like that old bird?

(Nursery Rhyme)

... Where is Silence? Nowhere but in the deep recesses of a stilled mind, cushioned on a perfectly serene emotional nature. Silence is not to be found on the surface of the outer world at all.

When you find Silence *inside* your Being, you can learn therein by experiment and practice to register the Voice of the Silence.

The hyperactive lower mind sees too much, speaks too much. It needs interludes of rest, for health; it needs interludes of Silence in which to learn to hear ...

Eventually, you learn to move at will into the depth of Being. In that state, the Spirit of the meditator communes with the Spirit of his God. In Silence, the Spirit in you invokes and evokes response.

Speak to Him thou for He hears, and Spirit with Spirit can meet –
Closer is He than breathing, and nearer than hands and feet.

(From Tennyson, The Higher Pantheism)

Margaret Rompage, 'Silence is a Noisy Place',
Communiqué, January 1989, (Sundial House)

Freed from deceptive activity, and from every guile, let the soul be collected, in silence. Let the soul that is not unworthy contemplate the Divine Soul.

Calmed be the body in that hour, calmed be the striving of the flesh. Let all that is anywhere about be calm. Calm be the earth, the sea, the air, as the heaven itself is still. Now let the soul experience how into a silent heaven the Divine Spirit floweth in.

Plotinus, *The Enneads*

At one time he [Apollonius of Tyana] kept silence for five years.

Sheldon Cheney, *Men Who Have Walked With God*

Molinos the Quietest Mystic gave as a formula for approaching the Un-nameable, 'Silence of the mouth, silence of the mind, silence of the will.' That silence, that allaying of the ego's tumult, that stilling of the waves of the mind is an art which needs every aid. Many, to whom visual symbolism is not a medium but a hindrance, not a lens but a thick stained glass window, would find in carefully applied music an instrument whereby to draw aside the flashing meshes of maya.

Gerald Heard, 'The Return to Ritual',
(From: *Vedanta for the Western World*)

... so many men and women of our day do not know how to rest, or even what real rest means. They are accustomed to constant movement and noise so that they are unable to keep still and endure silence. Here music comes to their rescue.

Roberto Assagioli, *Psychosynthesis*

The darkness of silence has to be penetrated before its final sequence, the passage of the soul to God, is traversed. The true 'cloud of unknowing' is the mystic's negative way to divine knowledge. As one enters the cloud, so all images are divested from one. One property alone remains, the power of love ...

The first use of silence is ... to explore the depths of our own personality, to come to terms with the fears and inhibitions that lie deeply placed in the unconscious part of the mind ...

The second use of silence is to be able to listen to what other people are actually saying to us ... When we are silent within we can, perhaps for the first time, begin to perceive the message of another person and listen to him with attention and concern ...

The third use of silence is to listen to what our lives are telling us about ourselves, to hear the voice of the Holy Spirit leading us into the truth of our condition ...

The end of silence is to rest in God, in whom alone is one's sustenance and life ... This silence is the precursor of prayer, the dialogue between the human soul and God.

Martin Israel, *Living Alone*

Few seek the peace within, because it is beyond their comprehension, being too young in evolution to have an inkling of its beauty and saving grace. Let us pray that the Light will illuminate their minds and hearts and souls when later they return here once more to try again.

Robert Fludd

As the personality becomes better integrated, so the soul within it makes its presence known ever more strongly. It becomes more articulate as we advance to the inner silence where the voice of God is heard. But in this silence other impressions enter our awareness also. These are from the extrasensory world that interpenetrates our own material one. In it float the fears and desires, the dejection and the aspiration, of all those in contact with us, and also those who have passed into the greater life beyond the grave . . .

Much of the psychic side of life emanates from dark forces in our own unconscious minds and those of other minds around us . . . The first point to be made is that *the soul is the organ of both psychical information and spiritual enlightenment.*

Martin Israel, *Summons to Life*

John Reuchlin said of Pythagoras that he taught nothing to his disciples before the discipline of silence, silence being the first rudiment of contemplation.

Manly P. Hall, *The Secret Teachings of All Ages*

The free will does not go into a state of restful oblivion and wait for God to do everything. This error, which is called quietism, leads to complete atrophy, or withering, of the personality. The free will brings the personality under the direction of the receptive soul, so that the inner voice can make its wordless message felt. And this message is one of strengthening, for indeed it is the Comforter (the bringer of strength) Who is the Holy Spirit . . .

Contemplation is the most exalted activity that man can perform. In it the whole personality is, under the action of the enlightened will, kept quiet so that the Holy Spirit can inspire it and lead it into greater truth. This apparently simple action of the will takes longer time to fulfil than we could bear to consider.

Martin Israel, Summons to Life

Subjugation of the mind is meditation: deep meditation is eternal speech. Silence is ever-speaking; it is the perennial flow of 'language'. Lectures may entertain individuals for hours without improving them. Silence, on the other hand, is permanent and benefits the whole of humanity . . .

By Silence Eloquence is meant. Oral lectures are not so eloquent as Silence. Silence is unceasing Eloquence . . . It is the best Language.

Bhagavan Sri Ramana Maharshi, Maharshi's Gospel
Books I and II

99

The spiritual ascent is, in essence, one of inner tranquillity in which we may become attuned to the voice of the soul within us. The inner stillness is not to be regulated merely to periods of prayerful meditation. Indeed, meditation can easily degenerate into a technique whereby we escape the threats and demands of an ever-challenging world. The stillness worth having is one that is with us in the clamour of the day's work.

Martin Israel, *Summons to Life*

In the exercise of mystical contemplation leave behind the senses and the activities of the intellect, and all things sensible and intellectual . . . that thou mayest arise, as far as thou mayest, by unknowing towards union with Him who transcends all being and all knowledge.

'Dionysius the Areopagite'
[Probably Bar Sudali, Syrian Monk]
The Mystical Theology

There are thinkers, not a few, who maintain that it is impossible to arrive at pure thought, free from any sensory content. These thinkers confuse what they feel bound to say about their own inner life with what is humanly possible. The truth rather is it is possible to arrive at higher knowledge only when thought has been liberated from all sensory content, when an inner life has been developed in which images of reality do not cease when their demonstration in sense-impressions comes to an end.

Rudolf Steiner, *Christianity as Mystical Fact*

If one is to approach God in silence, the mind must be still and at rest. When it is filled with all the world's commerce it cannot know the one thing that matters. When we speak of knowing, let us use that word in its archaic sense of having an intimate relationship with someone. We can only 'know' in this context when the mind is quiet and receptive . . .

The cultivation of inner silence is called meditation . . . despite the many teachers of the subject and the various techniques used, the minds of most people, even experienced meditators, are usually far from the centre where God is known. This is because the attitude and objectives of many of those who meditate are not centred on God but are devoted to the aggrandisement of the isolated self.

Martin Israel, *Summons to Life*

The 'negative way' – the way of 'unknowing' – is in reality based on an essentially positive insight. It is because of the immeasurable greatness and glory of God that He transcends our knowing. And 'unknowing' is in itself a positive attitude – the attitude of inner stillness which brings into play the deeper powers of the soul.

Sidney Spencer, *Mysticism in World Religion*

To a mind that is still the whole universe surrenders.

Chuang Tsu, *Chinese Texts*

A particular method of prayer, which has played a great part in the life of the Orthodox Church, was adopted by the monks of Mount Athos (in Macedonia) under the influence of St Simeon. The method, known as 'Hesychasm' (from the Greek hesychia or 'stillness') consisted in the practice of inner stillness or concentration of the mind on the divine Presence, induced by the repetition of the 'Jesus prayer' (O Lord Jesus Christ, Son of God, have mercy on me, a sinner), which was accompanied by controlled respiration – the prayer being repeated at each drawing of the breath ... This prayer culminated in the experience of ecstasy, in which men attained the vision of the divine Light.

Sidney Spencer, *Mysticism in World Religion*

What is the effect of this realization that the mind with all its contents is a thing that we use, not that we are? Does it mean that the inner man is left more and more attributeless – changeless, powerless, loveless, ignorant? It does not. In the process you are not divesting yourself of attributes but of limitations. The mind is swifter and freer than the body, and beyond the mind is the spirit, which is freer and swifter still. Love is more possible in the quietude of the heart than in any outer expression, but in the spirit beyond the mind it is divinely certain.

Ernest Wood. *Concentration*

There are three ways of holding one's peace in recollection, or three ways of silence . . .

The first is when all fantasy and imagination and forms of visible things cease in the soul, which is thus silent to all created things . . .

The second way of silence which is in recollection is that when the soul that is most still in itself enjoys a kind of spiritual ease . . .

The third silence of our understanding is brought to pass in God, when the soul is wholly transformed in Him and tastes abundantly of His sweetness, in which it sleeps as in a wine cellar, and keeps silence, because it desires nothing more.

Francisco de Osuna, *Third Spiritual Alphabet* XXI:4

Better is an handful with quietness, than both the hands full with travail and vexation of spirit.

Ecclesiastes 4:6

When the physical senses are hushed, and we begin to listen to that inner voice and surrender to it, we notice that moments of true healing and growth occur. In this silence, where the conflict of personalities has ceased to interest us, we can experience the joy of peace in our lives.

Gerald G. Jampolsky. *Love is Letting Go of Fear*

To be qualified for ... solitude, it is absolutely needful to observe that method recommended by the Psalmist, 'Commune with your own heart in your chamber, and be still.' 'Enter into thy closet, and shut the door about thee', says our Saviour ... And if the closet be not pleasant, the only reason is that it hath been less frequented than it ought ...

It is by silent and solitary study that the soul gets acquainted with the hidden mysteries of Scripture ... Think not then that the man who withdraws from his friends and acquaintances is perfectly alone. No, he only changes that for better company, and is visited in his quiet retreats by God and His holy angels.

Thomas à Kempis, *The Imitation of Christ*

If you are quiet and in a state of prayer when you turn, offering everything of yourself to God, then, when your body is spinning, there is a completely still point in the center. When you turn, all the stars, and the planets, and the endless universe turn around that still point. The heavens respond; and all the invisible kingdoms join in the dance.

[The Dervish 'Turn']
Reshad Feild, *The Last Barrier*. A Sufi Journey

At the still point of the turning world. Neither flesh nor fleshless. Neither from nor towards; at the still point, there the dance is. But neither arrest nor movement. And do not call it fixity. Where past and future are gathered.

Neither movement from nor towards, neither ascent nor decline. Except for the point, the still point, there would be no dance, and there is only the dance.

T. S. Eliot, *Burnt Norton* Section II:22

Delight is the secret. And the secret is this: to grow quiet and listen; to stop thinking, stop moving, almost to stop breathing; to create an inner stillness in which, like mice in a deserted house, capacities and awareness too wayward and too fugitive for everyday use may delicately emerge.

Alan McGlashan, *The Savage and Beautiful Country*

'The courts of sense we left behind' –
Thus the saints their story told –
'And in the stillness, yet more bold,
Passed beyond the mortal mind;
Beyond the mortal mind we passed –
Oh, listen well! –
Beyond the self, until at last
We came to THAT whereof no tongue can tell:
In a hidden place untrod,
Where death is dead, and grief unknown,
There, blissful on his royal throne,
We found the ATMAN – BRAHMAN – GOD!'

Frederick Manchester, Dedication Ode
(From: *Vedanta for the Western World*)

This control of the waves of the mind is not so simple as it would at first appear. It is a complete transformation of the character, when the mind becomes absolutely pure and tranquil. St Paul said: 'Be ye transformed by the renewal of your own mind.' That is it, and this control is the blessedness of purity which Jesus spoke of when He said: 'Blessed are the pure in heart for they shall see God'. He meant that complete transformation, that complete overhauling of the mind ...

Visions, spiritual ecstasies, occult powers are great in themselves, but there is a realm far beyond visions and ecstasies. Occult powers may come, but if you are tempted to use them, the door to spiritual progress is closed and you have to learn the secrets by which these powers can be controlled, and become once more a simple and humble seeker.

By transcending these powers and visions, the door to spiritual life is opened, and we experience samadhi, the transcendental consciousness. We come face to face with the Reality; then we can say with Christ, 'I and my Father are one'.

Swami Prabhavananda, 'The Yoga of Meditation'
(From: Vedanta for the Western World)

Through the regular practice of repeating the Holy Name the mind will gradually become tranquil ...

No more will the mind be troubled by the restless waves of lust and craving; by the power of the Word the mind becomes pure, transformed, renewed. Upon the pure mind the power of God descends. Unto the pure heart Reality is revealed.

Swami Adbhutananda, 'The Power of the Word'
(from: Vedanta for the Western World)

If so then you desire a safe stair and sure path to God, to arrive at the end of true bliss then with an intent mind earnestly desire and aspire after continual cleanness of heart and purity of mind with a constant calm and tranquility of the senses and recollecting of the affections of the heart, continually fixing them above . . .

So do until you become immutable and arrive at that true life which is God himself: perpetually, without any vicissitudes of space or time reposing in that inward quiet and secret mansion of the Deity.

Albertus Magnus (Albert the Great), *De Adherendo Deo*

Interior peace has many enemies. On the moral plane we find, on the one hand, anger, impatience and every kind of violence, and, on the other (for peace is essentially active and creative), every kind of inertia and slothfulness. On the plane of feeling, the great enemies of peace are grief, anxiety, fear, all the formidable host of negative emotions. And on the plane of the intellect we encounter foolish distractions and the wantoness of idle curiosity. The overcoming of these enemies is a most laborious and often painful process, requiring incessant mortification of natural tendencies and all-too-human habits. That is why there is, in this world of ours, so little interior peace among individuals and so little exterior peace between societies. In the words of the *Imitation*: 'All men desire peace but few indeed desire those things which make for peace.'

Aldous Huxley, 'Seven Meditations'
(From: *Vedanta for the Western World*)

It is unwise to discuss with strangers one's spiritual adventures unless it be an attitude of mutual helpfulness. Sooner or later one must learn not only 'to know' and 'to dare', but also 'to keep silent', and it will be well to learn at once the value of silence and occasional solitude.

Christmas Humphreys, *Concentration and Meditation*

You long for peace. You think of peace as being goodwill towards each other, goodwill among nations, the laying down of arms. But peace is far more than this, it can only be understood and realised within your heart. It lies beneath all the turmoil and noise and clamour of the world, beneath feeling, beneath thought. It is found in the deep, deep silence and stillness of the soul. It is the spirit: it is God.

White Eagle, *The Quiet Mind*

In order to prevent the mind from running after objects, a man must cultivate certain qualities in himself. These qualities are called in our Scriptures the Six Treasures. They are the true treasures of life. The first is tranquillity of mind, interior calmness, peace. Then comes sense control, mastery over your passions ... The third treasure is patience and forbearance. The next is burning faith in the ideal ... Then comes self-surrender. And finally, the freedom from the bondage of life.

Swami Prabhavananda, 'The Sermon on the Mount I' (From: *Vedanta for the Western World*)

Not the voice, but the vow;
Not clamour, but love;
Not the stringed instrument, but the heart,
Sounds in the ear of God.

From the Choir of St Damian, Assisi
(as recorded by Laurence Temple, *The Shining Brother*)

No sooner are the lips still than the soul awakes, and sets forth on its labours; for silence is an element that is full of surprise, danger and happiness, and in these the soul possesses itself in freedom.

Maurice Maeterlinck, *The Inner Beauty*

Observing silence cannot make a sage of one who is ignorant and immature. He is wise who, holding the scales, chooses the good and avoids the bad.

The Dhammapada 268:269

The Persian poet Saadi of Schiraz says ... 'Who knows God, is silent'.

Abraham Hayward, *Notes on Goethe's Faust*

In rising to the best in us, we rise to the Self in us, to Brahman, to God Himself. Thus when the sage of the Upanishads is pressed for a definition of God, he remains silent, meaning that God is silence. When asked again to express God in words, he says: Neti, neti, 'Not this, not this'; but when pressed for a positive explanation, he utters the sublimely simple words: 'TAT TVAM ASI', 'Thou art That'.

Juan Mascaro, *The Upanishads*
Introduction to the Penguin Classics Edition

Since an extra day is added in Leap Year the following is included to accompany it.

The Tibetans have a saying, 'Signs from the Soul come silently, as silently as the sun enters the darkened world.' And we must still ourselves and listen, so that we do not miss too much.

Michal J. Eastcott, *The Silent Path*

Index

112

113

114

115

116